'24-7'

Inclusion:

Crew Life:

Cruise Friendships

Book 2

Jackie Chase

CMV

'24-7'
Multi-Cultural
Workers Find
Diversity Recipe
to Heal a
Troubled World
Book 1

Jackie Chase

'24-7'
H.R. Guide for
"Inclusion"
See Books 1&2

www.inclusionPLUSdiversity.com

'24-7'
Inclusion: Crew
Life: Cruise
Friendships
Book 2

Jackie Chase

Three eBooks for Worker INCLUSION campaign

'24-7' Inclusion:

Crew Life:

Cruise Friendships

Book 2

Jackie Chase

AdventureTravelPress.com

'24-7' Inclusion: Crew Life: Cruise Friendships
By Jackie Chase
AdventureTravelPress.com, FL, USA
Copyright © 2019 by AdventureTravelPress.com

Ordering Information:
Quantity sales. Special discounts are available on quantity purchases by corporations, associations, and others. For details, contact the "Special Sales Department" at the E-mail addresses above.

'24-7' Inclusion: Crew Life: Cruise Friendships
By Jackie Chase
Color Print: ISBN 978-1-937630-47-8
eBook and Grayscale editions are available.

Publisher's Cataloging-In-Publication Data
(Prepared by The Donohue Group, Inc.)

Names: Chase, Jackie, author.
Title: '24-7' inclusion : crew life : cruise friendships /
    Jackie Chase.
Other Titles: 24-7 inclusion | Twenty-four-seven inclusion
Description: [Lady Lake, Florida] :
    AdventureTravelPress.com, [2019] | Series: '24-7' ;
    book 2 | Includes resources for further reading. |
    Print version issued with either color or black-and-
    white illustrations.
Identifiers: ISBN 9781937630478 (color print) | ISBN
    9781937630461 (grayscale print) | ISBN 9781937630454
    (ebook)
Subjects: LCSH: Diversity in the workplace. | Social
    integration. | Cruise ships--Employees--Interviews. |
    Tourism--Employees--Interviews. | Tourism--
    International cooperation. | Industrial relations. |
    LCGFT: Interviews.
Classification: LCC HF5549.5.M5 C432 2019 (print) | LCC
    HF5549.5.M5 (ebook) | DDC 658.3008--dc23

Crew keeping her ship shape

Contents

Foreword
To be completed by a company officer or board member

INTRODUCTION

This book shares a number of stories about fellow workers or crew members who live and work together aboard a floating resort. If you are part of any type of team, whether for profit, government, academic or charity, the stories will likely help you to perform better and perhaps help you advance in your chosen occupation. The stories will certainly show what life is like aboard ship, and why it takes a month or so to get comfortable working at sea; but it will also satisfy your curiosity about the many skills needed to be a success in the hospitality or any other industry.

The setting is the Columbus, one of a fleet of six cruise ships operated by Cruise and Maritime Voyages (CMV). The people interviewed range from old timers to new hires, and they simply tell about their lives, jobs and family, but they all have in common the desire to get acquainted with their fellow crew members who just happen to be from over a couple dozen countries. That makes for some interesting friendships and reading.

The stories describe the process of befriending people who are different; by the last page, you will remember a number of examples showing how you, too, might be able to greet someone, perhaps born in a foreign country or culture, or at least "different" in some way. If you are curious about the cruise business, you have many more reasons to want to peek beneath the waterline of a cruise ship and learn about the lives of those in this industry who have the pleasant task of pleasing passengers aboard ship.

Curiously, the benefits are not limited to large companies. One seafarer we know reported that his mom, a hairdresser, used the smile and greet friendliness and found her solo-worker business nearly doubled as a result. And this book reports many cases where promotions seemed to follow inclusion, teamwork, and leadership.

This ook, in traditional print , and eBook versions, shares stories from crew and management on how to deal with life aoard, and how to apply the golden rule of respect for others who may have quite different cultures from yours. The principles shared in this ook's crew comments are ap plicale to any group of people associated in any type of organization. They are intended to help the reader learn to ecome a etter representative for their employer and even their own families. Respect and smiles help the "smiler" as well as the "smilee"!

Your first introduction will be to the Captain! He is waiting for you to turn the page and start your exciting journey around the world.

CHAPTER ONE

🦅 *Master: Captain Ilias Venetantis: Greece*

I make sure the crew is well trained

What child has never dreamed of eing the Captain of an ocean liner? Imagine moving an entire floating city, with hundreds of residents, through the water, until the ship goes around the world and docks at the very spot the journey egan.

At age 14, Captain Venetantis ecame fascinated with sea life and adventure through sailing the world. As a teen, he worked on ferries and then entered the Merchant Marine Academy. He did well as a Deck Cadet on cargo ships and was promoted to Chief Officer. He earned a progression of steps to Captain of many types of ships.

One of the things to start off the ook for the crew might e if you would think in terms of talking to them aout what their life might e like the first few weeks and what kind of opportunities they might have?

Actually, that is

> *Total worldwide ocean cruise capacity at the end of 2018 was 537,000 passengers and 314 ships*

what we are doing for new crew members. We have the management introduction, and we do this ourselves. We give them a brief description of our roles, what is on board, and of course useful information. For some of them, it's a first time at sea and the first time on board, and it's very important information to know. I give them a brief description of what they need to pay attention to from my side, the Staff Captain's side and the Hotel Director's side.

"Do you talk to them about how they will be meeting people from many different cultures?"

We tell them that, especially for the crew, we are a multi-national, multi-cultural, and multi-religion environment. We have to work together in harmony and respect for each other. But I'm telling them, always respect. From the moment we respect others, they will respect us. This is a fundamental.

"And then do you ever give them any sense that you're a growing company, and there might be opportunities for promotion?"

They already know the company started with one ship a few years ago and now is growing, and they are getting soon another one. All of them know now that they have more opportunities for work.

"Do you think there are advantages to cultural diversity?"

It's a challenge. But, it's not the first ship with a multi-national environment. Nowadays all the ships are like that. The ships are getting bigger, and they need more people. And to find people you have to employ from different countries and cultures. It's not really a problem so far.

"Is it an opportunity to meet many people?"

Yes, of course. Sometimes we have events, like the Filipinos celebrate their Independence Day. The Indians have their Independence Day celebration with cake and invite the Senior Management team as well as all the crew. It is interesting to see different cultures, and somehow you are learning from this. Sometimes things from our culture mean different things for them. For us it's a special way of visiting different countries.

"How did your career get started?"

I started in 1979 as a cadet on cargo ships. In 1983, when I was already a chief officer on cargo ships, I found a chance to work on a cruise ship in Greece, and I stuck with it.

"What do you like about your job?"

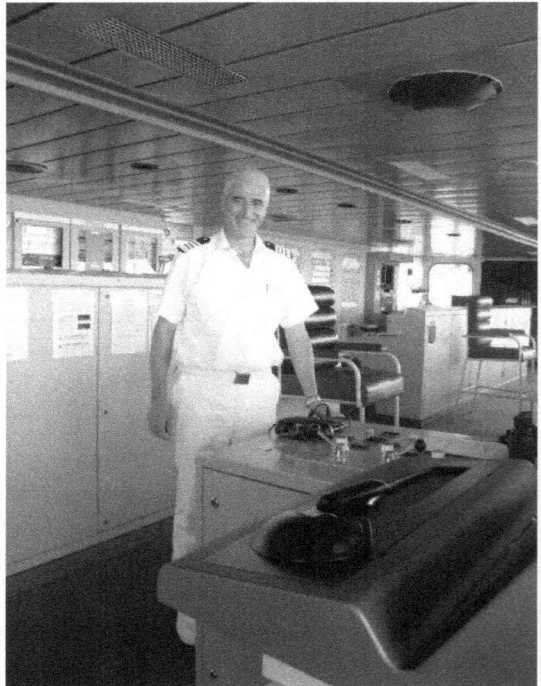

Captain Ilias Venetantis

First of all, I like the sea. To be honest, to do this profession, it is quite difficult. You are far from home and the people you love. You have to like the responsibilities. Especially my position's responsibilities. And with the cruise ships, you get the chance to socialize with many interesting people. You can go to many places cargo ships can't go. Of course, from the point of view of a much better life, the cargo ships sometimes face bad weather, and you see the same people for months.

"What is the hardest part of your responsibility?"

The hardest part is that, on my shoulder, I have 2000 souls. I have to be very careful. I have to make

First timer: Has this ship ever sunk?

sure crew is well-trained in case of emergencies and that the ship is safe.

"Any advice you would give to the young people coming aboard?"

For them, first of all to understand where they are, because it's a different environment than land. I know that they have free time to go out in port to see the places. Between their many duties, including safety, there will be free time to build a social life. Several months they are away from home, so they have to enjoy.

I don't think that many of them will have the chance at home to go to Papua, Bora Bora, or other places that are difficult to get to from their countries.

"When you go home what aspects of ship life do you miss?"

In the beginning, I want to relax because, from my point of view, the trip was quite successful, and I can start to relax. Then I start to miss again. I miss that we are active. That's why sometimes when Captains retire, they feel like a fish out of water. Doing nothing makes them feel uncomfortable.

"If you could have your favorite food dish brought on board, cooked by your mother or your wife, what would it be? What do you miss the most?"

What do I eat when I am going home? I prefer to eat some lentil soup or bean soup. I like simple, comfort food.

"Do you have a magic formula as to how to get along with people?"

I think it's the personality of a person; that helps us get along with others. It's not really any formula. It's something that you do, naturally. You have it or you don't. To continue in this profession, you really need to love it. Once you realize how much you like what you are doing, you really get into the job.

Master, Pilot, and Staff Captain on bridge wing

"There is a certain pride in going around the world?"

Yes, we are full of memories, and it's a nice feeling to know that you have been a part of it.

CHAPTER TWO

🎁 *Staff Captain: Taras Kompaniyets: Ukraine*

The deck hands appreciate me

Patience is the key. Leaders like this inspire confidence in crew. His door is always open for a friendly chat, to ask a question, or share a prolem. Not only

Introducing Officers

do his men work hard at keeping the decks painted and in tip top shape, ut Taras is most often seen in his coveralls, helping them.

"So, the crew would also like a small-size ship like passengers do?"
I often sit at the Captain's tale with guests for dinner , and what I have heard in comments always surprises me. I worked on ig ships for many years , and the passengers seem to like this size of ship. They say it's eca use it has such a warm atmosphere, and they are not disappointed with a lack of facilities.
,Are there a vanta es in the cultural iversity¡ Woul it e etter if everyone were from the same culture¡ "

Oh, that is a lon iscussion. It's always interestin , an what o you mean y etter¡ You mean more interestin or safer or more eneficial in services to the uest¡ What o you mean¡

So, if you ask me in the sense of safety, who knows when it comes to all the drills we do; we are playing some kind of scenarios, and yes, we are trying to improvise, ut still we simulate this and that. So, this is why the requirements are that everyody speaks enough English. Plus, in an emergency,

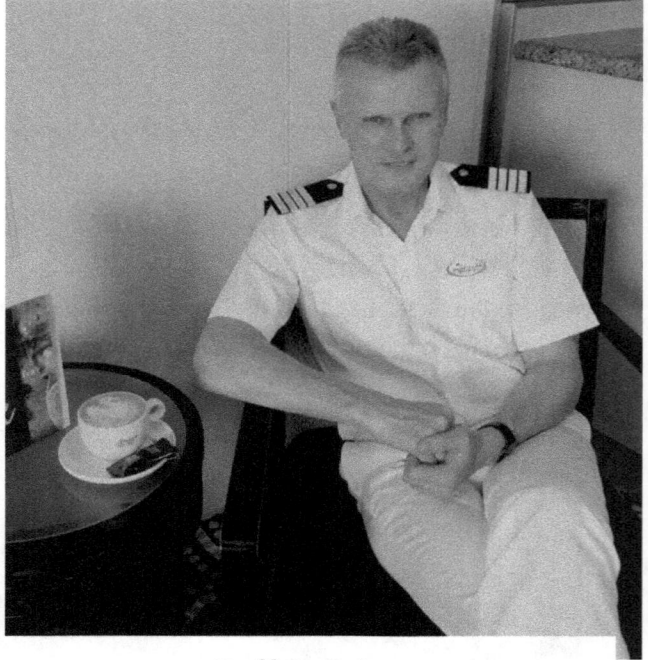

Staff Captain

everyody tends to use their own language.

"Have you ever thought when you are on vacation to go to someone's home who is in a different country?"

No not really, ut I was invited quite a few times. But I have not done it , and I don't know why. Maye one time in the US. Not for vacation , ut I was invited for some other reason. But it was as a guest, so I can say once. Kansas City.

"Is it your jo , when there are customs like in an eating situation, is it your responsiili ty to monitor that?"

Not really my responsiility. My responsiility is to deal with discipline issues like relationships, or someody goes to the front of the line disrespecting everyody in the whole line. Helping in arguments unfortunately is part of my jo. I also invite everyone to come and talk with me ; even though the suject doesn't relate to me, they still keep coming. I'm always trying to help, ut sometimes there are times when it's delicate. It depends on the personalities.

"What do you think you have learned from working on a ship?"

First of all, I have learne how to e patient. To e even more patient than I use to e , especially to e a mana er. The i er the ship you have, the more suor inates you have. An you are in comman . An there are all the nationalities, lan ua es, an sometimes haits. In some countries, for example, to e late for work is not a ig deal. Then you try to explain. When they say that it was only ten minutes, what's the point? You are trying to explain, and the guy doesn't understand and says again, it's not half an hour, it's just ten minutes, come on. So instead of getting mad, you have to express some kind of understanding which calms you down, so you ecome more patient.

> *I have an outside cabin; will I get wet if it rains?*

"It sounds to us like you really enjoy what you are doing."
I do. Sometimes it's a heavy load, ut the Captain also has a heavy load. Maye more than I do , ut his load is different than mine. I really like my position.

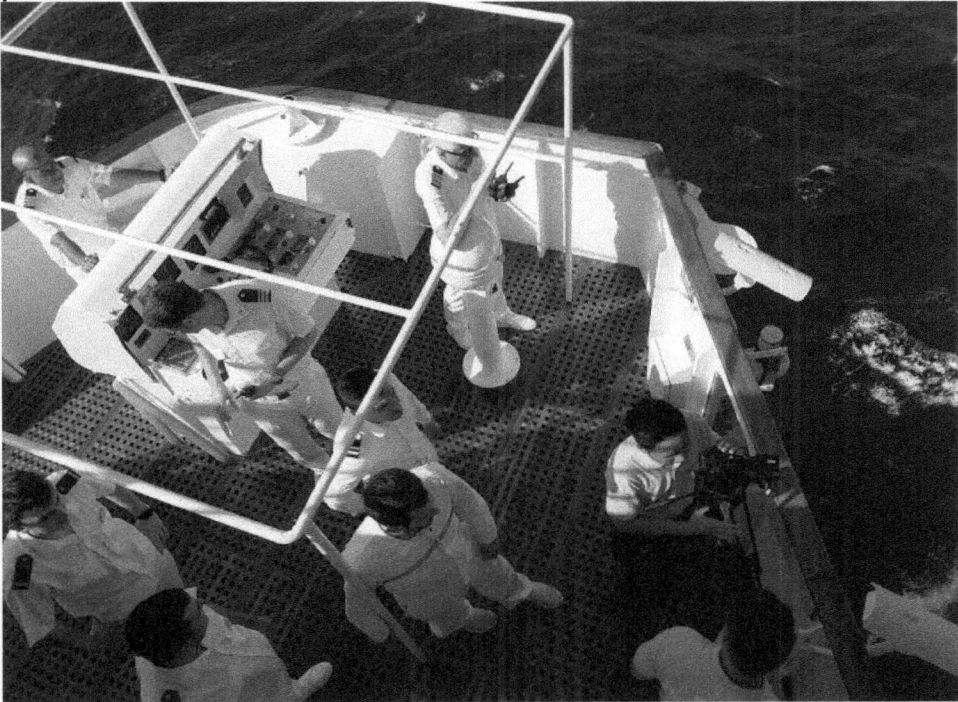

Crew on bridge wing

"You work more with the crew, don't you?"

First of all, I work as the head of the deck department. The deck department means those guys who work on the deck, like washing and painting to keep her nice. The engine room, food and housekeeping are another story. Our guys work on the deck, and they moor the ship, drop the anchors, and service the lifeoats. I am there with them , and they say, you are the first staff captain who doesn't wear the uniform. I like wearing the coveralls and eing right there eside them as they work. They really appreciate me eing there.

CHAPTER THREE

🦅 *Chief Engineer: Emmanouil Bouzounierakis: Greece*

We build a team and it's like a family

Some oys like toys. Toys that imitate the careers of those who dig asements with ig equipment, or plow and harvest grain, or lift   steel eams up to skyscrapers. An ocean-going ship is a very ig toy that stimulates the imagination of our youth: tomorrow's engineers.

A chief engineer is in the prevention and repair usiness. His summary includes things all crew memers should   understand.

I have 65 crew, including officers, under my supervision. We have meetings one to two times per week. In addition, there are separate departments from the engine department under my command including:

The Staff Chief Engineer who's in charge of main engine maintenance, various engine machineries and equipment, proper maintenance, and cleanliness of engine room, etc.

The Chief Electrician for electrical maintenance on engine rooms, various hotel equipment, lighting systems in pulic areas, open decks , etc.

The Hotel Engineer for mechanical maintenance of various equipment and machineries in galley, laundries, and also for maintenance of life oats, davits, etc.

The AC Engineer for maintenance of air conditioning on oard, ventilation, fan

Chief Engineer, Emmanouil Bouzounierakis

rooms, refrigeration system, cold rooms, and various types of fridges and ice makers on galleys, cains, pulic areas, etc.

They have daily meetings on their respective work stations or workshops to provide and give all work orders to their crew.

"Who provides the tools and parts?"

On oard, we have engine store rooms managed y Engine Storekeepers where all spare parts, tools and special tools for all machineries and equipment are placed and organized on shelves, cainets, and oxes. The Engine Storekeeper is responsile for providing spare parts and tools to the crew and ordering of spares to maintain and replenish stocks. All officers/supervisors are monitoring their spare parts and tools and advising the Engine Storekeeper for orders, and it's my responsiility to check and do the final approval.

"Is it possile to say how much fuel is used?"

It depends on the speed, load, and how many engines are running.

"What kind of schooling did you have efore you came into the field?"

I studied Marine Engineering, and during that year of schooling, I went to night school, ecause I needed to work in the morning to earn money so I can provide all my necessities, and help myself to finish my course.

"Does anyody ever get hired at a port to come on oard and fix something?"

Yes. On some occasions, we're requesting or hiring persons/technicians for some machineries or equipment that cannot e fixed onoard.

"Is there anything special that you do for your people?"

Yes. By veral compliments, we give them motivation and minimize the pressure of their jos. Every week, I'm giving some rest time to my crew and officers. It depends on the conditions or if it is not a usy day. But, of course, we are still standing y at all times in case of emergency. Also, I am giving them the opportunity to go ashore and enjoy the port to release their stress. But, most of my staff want to go ashore. For this reason, we are organizing the time for everyone to make sure that someody will stay to handle or relieve their duties and responsiilities in case of emergency. For this reason, I elieve they are happy.

"What aout women in the marine side?"

In the maritime industry, most of the women are working in the hotel department, ut in some cases, you will encounter a few women working in the deck or engine areas. Our department has heavy work and jos that simply cannot e handled y a woman's ody. That's the reason why in our department, we are all men.

"There must e a lot of prolems that you have, ecause you're confined."

Yes, that's true. Our jo on oard is not so glamorous as people think. We encounter some prolems which give us stress , and we feel tired, ut it's part of our duties and responsiilities and , in spite of our heavy jos, it is a very satisfying jo, and we do love our jo. I have een working on ships from 1988. So many good memories, and I end up liking my jo emotionally.

Do you get out and watch people working?"

Yes, especially for important matters, heavy jos, and emergency situations to

Mechanic catching up on reports

secure the safety of my crew and the safety of the ship.

"What do you like est aout your jo?   What part of it is the most interesting to you?"

Well, after so many years, there are no surprises. What is interestin is that there are always new people in my life, an we uil   oo relations, make frien s, an have happy memories. I love workin with my team. I like to work on the engine. I have a first engineer for that. I can trust my har -workin crew, an they trust me. We uil a team, an it's like a family, an for me, that is the most interestin part of our jo.

CHAPTER FOUR

🦅 *Hotel Director: Allwyn Furtado: India*

I always have smiles to hand out, which makes it a happy ship

We know that a hotel is a place to stay for a day or a month or more, but what about managing a hotel that circles the globe? Some of the issues are quite different for the crew that plans to please over a thousand guests for a long voyage. That's Allwyn's job.

"Do you think there is an advantage to the cultural diversity on the ship?"

Yes, we have an impressive range of different cultures from

> *The UK cruise industry provides 70,000 jobs.*

around the world on board. From day one, new employees are eager to make new friends and learn the different languages, values and behaviors of their new colleagues and housemates/neighbors. Many people pursue a life at sea with the simple ambition to travel the world, yet what they find along the way is that they have made friends and memories that will last a lifetime.

Life at work on a cruise ship offers a unique experience and environment that allows its employees to learn and grow – and that makes me proud.

"And when did you start?"

I first dipped my toes into the cruise industry on the 23rd of November 1997 as a bar utility with Festival Cruise Lines. My main roles were to assist and support the bar tenders in their role by ensuring that alcohol, mixers, clean glasses, ice and garnishes are all clean and on hand, ready to be served.

My father was my inspiration for pursuing a career at sea, as he too worked on ships for many years. As a boy, I was thrilled to receive handwritten letters from my father's life and adventures at sea. My father had fantastic handwriting; whilst at sea he kept a diary of the friends he made and the ports where he docked, and so, I did this too, on a computer file named "My Journey".

"What message do you want us to share with people?"

When I introduce myself to new crew members, I always try to encourage them to give 100%, to focus on their goals, and to aim towards reaching higher because the benefits of a career at sea are incredible.

Always a smile in Allwyn's pocket

As for my guests, I wish to keep them happy and to provide them with an experience of a lifetime when they cruise with us. On board, we work like a family, and the guests are such an important part of our job, we want them to feel welcome to cruise again with us in the future.

This company began with just one ship, the Marco Polo in 2009, and without our wonderful, supportive guests and our fantastic family of staff and crew, both on board and ashore, we would not have grown and evolved into the fleet of six ships which we have today. I continue to be impressed by the CMV workforce; it is clear that a lot of hard work, dedication, and perseverance has gone in to building this company.

"Are there opportunities for promotion within CMV? And are employees encouraged to strive for promotion?"

Yes, of course. Our current Bar Manager, Elvis, joined the company in the sanitation department as a utility person. Gabriel is currently our Chief Housekeeper, yet he began his career as a Cabin Steward. Myself, I joined the company as an Assistant Bar Manager in 2009; by 2017 I was given the opportunity to be Hotel Director on Magellan. I find it really inspiring to see familiar faces that I have met along my journey, working really hard and achieving their goals and getting that promotion.

Here at CMV we support the initiative and ambition of our team members; I believe it is important to nurture the creativity within a team as it will help to provide a more diverse set of solutions that can be adapted to deal with different specific situations.

"How do you make crew members with small representations on board feel at home, for instance, Nepal?"

With close proximity to India, most of the Nepalese are adapted to our living standards, so it is not difficult for them to acclimatise. For smaller groups like Georgia, we encourage them to put

> *She asked us if passengers in 'outside cabins' get extra blankets to stay warm at night.*

forth their culture by way of food. We ask if they would like to cook a local or their national dish for the crew members to sample Georgian food.

This is a popular way to boost camaraderie on board. We would never isolate people based on their nationality; we continuously take on the challenges and devise methods to do things right. It is useful to review and adopt the resolution techniques used with our guests and apply it to crew members as well. With a growing fleet that is expanding into new markets and countries, we are constantly learning and adapting our environment so that everyone feels welcome.

With the introduction of our Crew Ambassador position two years ago, challenges have significantly reduced. Elian, The Director of Operations, along with Jakob said that 'We need a Mother Teresa on board', and that is how the idea of having a Crew Ambassador was created.

Here on Columbus, it was decided that the Crew Ambassador position should be one that does not wear stripes, to keep the position neutral and the person approachable. Ritesh is the Crew Ambassador on board Columbus; he works relentlessly liaising between the crew, the Cruise Director and the Staff Captain to create an open and comfortable environment.

"Do you think there is some kind of magic that helps you shine? What gives you that extra spark to work with strangers and always be happy?"

You always need to be happy; the ship is made of steel and wood, but the heart of the ship is its crew. Nobody wants to be sad or see an angry face, so I always carry small, paper-cut-out smiles in my pocket; that way, if I get caught without a smile, I can assure them that someone is always smiling here.

After being in the industry for more than twenty years, my heart will always be with the crew. I have done the jobs that they are doing; they know that I have been in their shoes earlier in my career. Wherever I am on the ship... it's the greetings, the high fives, and the smiles that indicate that the crew is happy, and that makes me realise I am doing a good job for my family on board. I have never had a problem with the ratings in the last three years, and that is because I am on a happy ship... and it all starts with the crew.

CHAPTER FIVE

🦅 *Safety Officer: Konstantinos Triantis: Greece*

Charity begins with a tsunami

He exhiits a   high degree of nautical competence. Sailors with that kind
of careful proficiency possess a quality that might e called sea   sense,
which is essentially a lending of common sense with seamanship.   Safety is
not assumed on any ship.

"What are the responsiilities   of a Safety Officer?"

As safety officer on oard,   I'm third in command. I have responsiility
for the firefighting equipment and lifesaving equipment maintenance, and I
show the crew how to participate.

I make training for the crew to react in case of on-oard emergencies,
like the main cases of emergency, such as fire, and I also advise aout the
things they shouldn't do and remind them of their duties to understand. I
plan suitale training accordingly. We don't want to have any ad
situations.

"What is it like working with so many different nationalities?"

Actually, it's hard. Many people support the utilization [of many
cultures], ut for me, I'm a little it opposite: in case of emergency, what
language do you use? Very often you talk directly in your mother language.
At the last ig tragedy with Costa Concordia, they did record the
conversation of the Captain in his first orders. What he said was in the
Italian language, accidentally. Of course, there are standards from
headquarters in Greece. I have a ifferent accent with the En lish lan ua e,
  ifferent from you in the Unite States. Different from my collea ues from
Romania,   ifferent from Chinese. Everyo y is suppose to know En lish,
ut even that lan ua e ives us many prolems.

This is the second point. People have a different modality, a different
philosophy of their life. We respect this.

"Do you think there are prolems with too many nationalities working
together?"

For safety reasons, the Bridge should have no more than two
nationalities. Ideally, there cannot e more than two nationalities [for
rescue teams]. In case of emergency, they have to accommodate a common
language to react very fast. In cains, we'll have one cain with full crew
insi e; one is In ian, one is Ukrainian, another one is a Romanian, an the

fourth one is from In onesia. We try for the est, an they learn to et alon , on't they¡

"Yes, they have to respect each other!"

That is the main point that not only is for the oo ; I think it's also for our relationships. I hol to that octrine. I say to all the roups, on't respect me for my rank. First of all, you respect me as a person.

"So, do you teach them aout certain customs and traits? Customs are emedded in people their whole life."

They've lived with certain ways of doing things. They are silent sometimes, ut sometimes we see in it all the prolems.

Safety is always first

"Do you try to change the jos if the person would do etter in another jo?"

My jo is part of the human management. It's not only for my jo, ut all heads of departments. They should know and understand this. Of course, I give a different jo to a seaman when he's, for example, 60 years old. First of all, I respect his age. We see his possiilities, and we want to keep as many people as we can. When you are over a certain a e, we throw you a ifferent, let's say, part of the jo. We nee to o this from our human point of view. Young people may come without visas, without dreams, without targets. They come for money. I pray sometimes when I elieve this person has potential .

"Do your people do random act of kindness?"

We hear of many traumatic stories. I hear stories too when they have, for example, a tsunami in Asia; we collect money for them an for the families. Officer Triantis was proud of the charitale attitude of the crew.

CHAPTER SIX

✿ Maître de Hotel: Reynaldo Obumani: Philippines

Have a vision for something next year and the next

Opening the doors to the dining room are the staff memers who know how to make your evening start with a smile. They welcome you with open arms and

Reynaldo is ready to help

smiled greetings. There is no dout that restaurant management is a profession. So, you hire a professional who knows all the angles. Reynaldo is assistant to the restaurant manager, and supports that manager including all the functions of the uffet, crew mess, tale allocation, pulic hygiene, and staffing. His career egan in 1998.

"What do you do with the waiters and assistant waiters? Do they look to you for guidance?"

Those in management train the supervisors; then the supervisors train the wait staff. If there is an issue, they need to work with the supervisor. If they can't find a solution for the issue or a prolem, Reynaldo will try his est to solve it. Mostly there is no issue, only a misunderstanding. Misunderstandings can start from different nationalities ecause of the varied cultural haits, like the tone of their voice or the diction.

Accents are different. So Asian people like me sometimes are sensitive to that, and I have a feeling for this, ecause I used to work with the different nationalities since 1998. However, if you are new on oard, it's hard. It's very hard to resolve this kind of situation; numer one is the attitude and likes, dislikes, and tone of voice. We put similar accents (same nationality) together in wait staff assistants where possile , who can speak very well in English with anyone in most cases. Good communication is helpful to run the restaurant, especially for the waiter taking the order.

"It's etter for everyone if there are fewer cultures working closely together?"

On the other hand, no cruise line works well with only one culture. That's not good either. You can enhance and improve your guest interaction with various cultures.

We have to e oo in En lish communication. These are the challen es that we always encounter, ut for the work, it oe sn't have any issue. Asian people an other cultures work har , ecause they love the jo. Some people , like a European, think that it's easy for them. I ha never worke with Myanmar crew efore, an once you see them improvin an enhancin their skills, you know you have tau ht them the ri ht way.

> Are there islands completely surrounded by water?

"Can you tell with your experience that this particular person is going to move up ecause they've got real potential?"

I can feel if your attitude is not good enough for me; attitude is very important to me.

"Have you seen friendships develop etween nationalities?"

In my case, I treat people the same. Fair and square. Everyody is my friend. However, after the service operation, this is the free time to chat with somedy else, and they can share their thoughts .

Every night we have a riefing. We start with a joke, ecause it's the only thing that can ring them together, so close. To like the jo, there are a lot of factors.

On my side, I always mention that you're here for your family; love your jo, and it will e a nice goal that takes care of itself over time. Yes. If you are contented with what you have now, e thankful, and wait for the next step. I always mention to them, you're still young, and so you will work.

For my supervisors, I've always tol them, share your knowle e. Don't e ree y. It's the same with the waiter. That person will replace you, an then you o up, an they will never for et, ecause you tau ht them the oo i eas. So, they have a vision for somethin next year an the next year.

It's hard, ecause they're thinking right now, what I have to do is hard work. But there's something in the future. You want the good ones to come ack for another contract. That's why I'm here. I don't like to lose them, ecause they are experienced. Promotin is very important. In here, the crew are like my ki s. Without them, I cannot survive, an without me, they on't

Waterfront dining staff ready for first seating

know the next function. Sometimes there's a mistake, ut we are not perfect. Everyo y makes a mistake. If you care, you'll et them ack. I'm not here to work only ut to ive them i eas.

Before you respect the other person, you nee to respect yourself first. And if you have a prolem ack home, tell your supervisor. And manage rs need to watch the expression on the face, the way people move, and if I see that look, I call their supervisor to take them aside and ask if everything is okay? Ask them if they are happy, and if not, tell them to go ack and rest and you will see them tomorrow. I always mention family. I'm always sharing with them, ecause we are all so far from our families.

"If you have experienced what they are going through, it helps them?"

Yes, I am here to correct what needs to e corrected. And it all comes from the heart. I care a lot, which is why I push the idea that you love your family, so work hard; save as much as you can.

Briefing before guests arrive

CHAPTER SEVEN

🦅 Doctor: Roberto Teru: Romania

Our skills are a gift

There is a doctor in the house! The following is a condensed version of his mission. His first task is to take care of all passengers and crew from a medical standpoint, including sanitation that could impact disease,

Keeping the ship healthy

especially that which could e contagi ous.

His main jo is to e sure that everyody on the ship is healthy, including the crew of 600. He hopes all coming aoard will e healthy. Sometimes   a crew memer doesn't feel well, and their supervisor has to know why the crew memer is disappearing . He logs into his paperwork all information, and then the crew memer is seen y the doctor,   diagnosed, treated, and sent ack to

Ready for medical emergencies

his supervisor. The department head is also notified so they know this crew memer has a medical prolem.   A cold or ack pain is the most common prolem.

We don't want the passenger to have any additional stress. People don't come here to visit the hospital, ecause they don't have anything else to do. They are really sick and need medical advice or treatment. The six hospital eds are normally not occupied to capacity.

Yes, I like working here, and I'll tell you why. I have a wife and child; so, it's hard, ut I used to work in the emergency room. I would work a 48-hour shift

without going home at all. So now, I prefer to e five or six months on
oard. Then , after that, I can stay at home and fully enjoy my family
without a worry someone will call with an agenda.

I like the challenge of working on the ship and the possiility to
diagnose and deal with the case. At home, a doctor would stailize the case,
suggest a diagnosis, and send them off to the cardiologist or whatever.
Now, I can do all these things y myself. First you take the emergency;
second, stailize the patient; third treat the patient; and fourth, follow up.

I may not have some fancy tools and equipment, and sometimes I feel
like it's not enough. But I can do a lot of things.

"When you have to life-flight someone off the ship, do you make that
decision?"

Yes, noody could judge etter than me when I have the patient right in
front of me. I do inform the nearest land location ecause this is an
elaorate procedure. Sometimes, you have to alter the course of the ship.
Phone calls and paper work go along with all the other arrangements. A
helicopter generally operates as far as 150 miles from land.

"If you are coming to a new port and have a patient in your hospital
ward, do you automatically move them to the land hospital?

No, unless it's something we cannot handle here. It's not how many days
that they can stay here on oard ; it's y the complexity of the case.

"What tasks do you enjoy doing the most? Do you like the thinking cases
where you have to take a lot of time to figure out what is wrong?"

The doctor says, I don't like it easy. Everyody can do easy. I am happy
you opened the suject. I'm a hard worker.

But there's another a vice which I will ive. I want to ive for other
people, octors, nurses, whatever. Just keep a low profile. Now, what o I
mean y that; I mean , on"t take it for rante that you are the est ,
ecause you have come up with experience , an just keep that low profile.

Because I stron ly elieve

| Do the crew members sleep on board? |

that all of us, we are just tools
in Go 's han s, an that it is
just a ift, an you have to use it properly. Sometimes you do ask for a
second opinion, which is often needed for insurance reasons.

"When you do get off the ship and go on an excursion as an escort, then
what happens if there is an emergency?"

I don't go so often, only when a lot of people are going like 900 people
to Petra. It's not a pro lem in port, ecause we are always in contact with
the local hospital.

CHAPTER EIGHT

❦ *Financial Controller: Helen Demostenis: India*

I help people from the heart

One way to learn aout an organization is to talk to its people. Let's listen to what Helen has to share as her philosophy aout many things that might e helpful to the reader.

"Tell us aout your jo."
I am the financial controller in charge of all the accounts on oard including the passengers as well as the crew plus the crew salaries. I have a team of two who are handing crew matters. The other one handles clearances in a port along with the documentation. I have an accountant who is assisting me with the reports I have to prepare. I am also in charge of the IT department who takes care of all the networking.

"How long have you een working on ships?"
I have een working since 1999.

"How to you feel aout the cultural diversity? Is it a plus?"

We are learning every day

I feel it is a plus. When we have ifferent nationalities for everyone, it wi ens your perspective. You et to know the culture of other people, their haits. There may e some nationalities who are not as hospitale as those in our hospitality areas, ut then you see other good points, and you learn from them.

When you are REALLY hungry!

Our industry is all ased on hospitality. I'm originally from India, ut I have a Portuguese nationality. I've noticed some ladies ack home, it's a different upringing, a different way of thinking compared to some European women who are very strong. They learn from other nationalities and put ideas together.

You know, like when you have a situation, how everyone rin s up their i eas. Because I also elieve in not just oin everythin on my own. It's very important to ele ate. That's how you have a epartment, an people rin in their i eas. You then choose etween which is the est , an which is the most efficient an easiest for everyo y. I elieve in iversity.

We have to appreciate everything that we have. If we have good health, we have the air to reathe for free and food to eat.

And we are safe, not in war-stricken countries. And we have a jo. I cannot

| Why are the ruins in such bad condition? |

complain. I think I'm one of those luckiest people and among the happiest and richest people on earth.

, Have you seen any en er prolems in the cruise in ustry¡ "

Not really. I never face this prolem. In fact, I was always appreciate for my i eas or whatever I rou ht to the mana ement. This company has een fair for the past 11 years, an I woul n't e here if I i n't have these won erful osses in the hea off ice. The CEO was in hotel operations earlier. They have always een supportive. I really enjoy workin here.

I elieve that mine is just a position. The minute I'm on the gangway I'm just Helen. I help people from the heart. They respect the person, not just ecause I'm wearing the stripes.

"What tips do you have to reak down the arriers of cultural hait and traditions. What works for you?"

You have to e open minded to accept ideas, ecause if you're closed with your own way of thinking, you can e her e for 20 years, and you'll still e with the same mentality. You cannot change someone else. You have to e ready to change yourself.

So first you open your perspective to accept new i eas. Learn. We are learnin every ay until the ay we ie. No one is a superstar, an noo y's perfect. The minute you

28 million people cruised in 2018.

open up an chan e yourself, I'm sure everythin aroun you will chan e, ecause then you look at thin s in a ifferent way.

"It's like a channel flowing inward toward you. You're now open to all those possiilities?"

In In ia we have so many reli ions, an the people live in peace. We on't have a prolem with each other. It's only the overnments an the politicians who make these issues for their own veste interests.

My est friend is a Hindu. I have very good relationships with some Muslims, and they are our family and friends; they'll always help you. We live in harmony. Not everyody thinks alike. Some people have a narrow mentality: you cannot do anything aout them. You just have to let them go. Just let them e the way they want. I think sometimes you want to give love, and people can change. They say if you squeeze an orange, you will only get orange juice. You cannot get apple juice.

Whatever is inside you will always come out, ecause I see such eautiful energy flowing out of people, and I am ale to receive this love and speak out. I et my oo thou hts from my elief. I am not ju in any other reli ion as I am very open. I have my partner who is a Muslim. I have two eautiful children. My eldest son is 21 years old. I look and feel young ecause of happiness. I appreciate everything that I have. In everyody's life, the difficult phases do come, ut then you always think in one year's time it'll e nothing. You always learn something positive from the difficult. It makes you stronger all the time.

At that moment, you just feel completely down, completely locked off. Then help comes into the picture.

They sai no one can harm you with their wor s. Only when you accept it an   react o you harm yourself. I'm always trying to connect my children with the reality of life and to let them know how lessed they are.   Children today can get lost, especially if they don't have their mother or father near them. But I may have done something good in this life, ecause my children are angels. I don't take the credit for eing a   good mother; I give it to my mother who is my rock. She has always stood y me and is my guardian angel.

"What is your advice for younger people coming a oard the ship? What is the path to move upward?"

First thing is to e eager to learn. Very important, ecause the more you learn, the more you grasp, ecause you don't know everything. Especially when you're new. You have to e open to learn, given the hours

> Anchors weigh as much as four elephants.

needed, ecause you need to work hard to get t o where you are. An   e frien ly with people; this is very important, ecause you can reak so many wron   impressions y ein frien ly with someone. Sometimes your face may say somethin , an   when you actually speak to the person, you   et to know the person etter. It's a   ifferent impression.   Be careful with your money; invest wisely, ecause sometimes , when you come from other countries, you think everyone is here for the money. But we have families ack home.

I'm always looking at someone else who's in a worse situation than me, and I see I'm lessed.   Our children are our main concern for us parents. If our children are set, it's like they will always e children even when they are grown. I think it's very important to show them the reality of life. When we work a oard,   we can afford to give them extras, and then they don't know what is life. May e   it's my way of thinking, ut I h ave never struggled a lot. I look at someone else who is in a worse situation than me and feel lessed.   Be open to all new thin s, ecause it is the only way to   row.

CHAPTER NINE

Cruise Director: Iain Bagshaw: England

We try to make people laugh

"How does it feel working with strangers all the time and working in the pulic?"

Yes, it's very good ecause you meet a lot of people every sin le ay. It's fascinatin to see where people are from.

"What are the secrets to meld all the cultures together into one team?"

Cruise Director loves to juggle

People get hired for their roles as a singer, musician, or me as the man in charge of the entertainment team. Keep a happy atmosphere, and lead y example. I don't expect anyody to do anything I wouldn't e prepared to do.

Be firm, ut fair. I on't micromana e people too much. If I nee to e firm I will e. The uys support my team an create an atmosphere where people are happy. I've een in entertainment for a long time and started as a magician and discovered a skill I didn't know I had.

"What do you think makes you shine. What motivates you?"

To give a good show, and to make the people happy motivates me. Whether it e doing my magic or hosting a game show, I do it to the est of my aility. Ultimately the guests who are watching it want to have a good time. My style is to try an make people lau h so I o silly jokes an make it as much fun as possile.

He fools the eyes with card tricks

CHAPTER TEN

🦅 *Guest Services Manager: Alistair Sellers: UK*

We don't say 'no'

Any hospitality industry manager who is serious about pleasing people needs a very patient and competent staff and a friendly set of guidelines to set the tone for a service-oriented mission.

"What is your mission?"

On a daily basis, I, and the Hotel Director, work very much together on what's happening with the hotel, and what's happening with the passengers. The Hotel Director is in charge of the whole hotel operation, and the next one down is the Guest Services Manager.

Hospitality is the product that we offer. My focus is the customer services side. I'm dealing with everything that's going on. It could involve cabin issues or any service issues. I work closely with the department heads, and I have a very strong relationship with them. They are the housekeeping manager and restaurant manager. All deal with guests on a day-to-day basis; the service to passengers is my main focus, and to make sure that the product is being delivered, and that we all work closely together. The Hotel Director has to focus a bit more on the food and beverage operation and also behind the scenes with provisioning.

But he relies on me to take care of "front of the house" administration, or anything that falls under my jurisdiction. The overall goal of this position is to make sure that the product is being delivered to the passengers. You can never

Guest Services Manager Alistair

100% satisfy everyone. You try your best. We can't do anything about the

weather and other circumstances out of our control like the sea conditions. Anything could happen, and you just have to find solutions, and deal with what comes up.

"How does cultural diversity affect all of this?"

With respect to cultural diversity, there are different nationalities on board. We work very well together. We've got those from Eastern Europe, Asia, and all kinds of people from different countries. We all gel very well together. I think everybody has the same attitude and the same mentality that we're here to serve the guests. We're here to do a job.

It's vitally important that we all work together; otherwise it won't work. I think that culture is good. It goes all the way through the ship. It doesn't matter whether it's me or somebody who's working in the galley or behind the bar; we're all on the same wave length, and we're all here to do the same job. And then we all look at each other as equals as well. Obviously on board a ship, you have a hierarchy.

I treat everybody as I would want to be treated. Even though I might be in a higher position, I will be interacting with and talking to them. We are one team, and we work together and want people to be happy and to enjoy their jobs as well. It's also important that we project a very happy team-working environment.

> 86% of cruise passengers are college/university graduates

The diversity is absolutely fine. We've got so many nationalities. We're having a lot of people now coming from other cruise lines that have had crews for quite a few years. We are attracting workers, and they're coming over.

We offer the traditional style of cruising: adults only. That's a very big thing. A lot of our passengers, they've had grandchildren, they've had children, and it's not that they don't like them, but when they want to come away on a holiday and relax, they want to be in an environment where it's people of a similar age; and they can be much more relaxed without children or teenagers.

I've discovered this cruise line feels like it has heart. It doesn't treat everybody like a commercial customer. We treat everybody like an individual and give them more than the average cruise line.

"Do you suggest you are going the extra mile?"

Yes, we try to go the extra mile. We emphasize to the staff that there's no such word as 'no'. I think over the years that has been forgotten, but we try and push our staff there. We might not be able to offer it, but there's a way of telling that to a guest, like let me look into it. Let me find out.

"Let's say you have a person from a certain nationality from the Philippines or wherever, and the passenger has a problem. Have you ever brought in somebody from the crew from that nationality to talk to them so that they can communicate, knowing their background?"

Most definitely. I've had cases before where we've even needed Spanish; for example, we have a guest that only speaks Spanish. When they booked the cruise they wanted, they were very interested in the traditional British style. And then they like the cruising, but they were obviously under the assumption that, as on some of the huge cruise liners, they had different translators, and they're available permanently.

"Are there incentives to help your staff really excel other than just money?"

We have now introduced a Crew Ambassador, and that person puts together a daily program for the crew and organizes activities for them. That's not just on the ship; that's also ashore. And they coordinate with our shore excursions team to see if a shuttle bus could be organized, maybe on a certain occasion. A big thing we offer is

> A ship moving at 20 knots is moving the same as a land vehicle moving 23 miles per hour

"Employee-of-the-Month" It's about you as a whole, but involves your supervisor. The guests might love you. Then, with your responsibility, you might be late quite often; the Employee-of-the-Month is a package rewarding a good all-round employee who goes the extra mile, is good with the passengers, is always on time completing everything correctly, and then the department heads will select them.

Star-of-the-Month is more what the guests think. The guests have a little card in their cabin, and you can write down names; if there is somebody that has gone the extra mile for you, you can vote for them. There are things in place to give motivation. It's helpful to actually be praising them. I think sometimes that gets forgotten as well. We tend to do more now in praising our crew. Well done. Good job. Thank you. Managers might get a bit of extra compensation here and there, but really, it's about delivering the service to the guests. If you get somebody turned around, and they say "thank you very much, that was brilliant", or writes a letter or sends something into the head office and compliments you; that is your bonus and your finance commission in this business.

"One thing we have noticed about CMV in talking to everybody is that it seems like you hire the right people?"

And they have a curiosity about their fellow crewmates, so what you are selling is variety in life. It's like going back to college. They've given you all different kinds of plates to sample. When you go home, you are a richer person.

For the guests, it's all about the learning, and they learn these things from the lectures. They meet different people and make friends. Then they go home, and they keep in contact with each other, and then they end up cruising together.

"We think the crew ambassador idea is working out very well."

> I bought an ocean view room, and all I can see is the parking lot?

Yes, it shows we value the crew and want to do something for them. And also, on their off time, they need to know what to do and where to go. Like the guests get their daily Explorer newsletter, the crew get their own daily paper. The crew ambassador gets ideas from the crew, and that helps them a lot.

"When you see unusual effort on somebody's part, where they're going out of the way or doing something extra, do you try to promote them and encourage them?"

We encourage cross-training and internal promotions, especially the lower down positions.

Definitely promotions from positions can be done internally. You could have a hotel trainee that moves into being a receptionist, and the receptionist could be very skillful and work hard, and then they could go up to a senior receptionist position or something more diverse in the back of the house, like program coordinator or a printer.

This is just the administration side. Then, with the restaurants, you'd be joining as junior waiter and then to senior. There is promotion from within. I think it's good to promote from within, because they know the product more. The people they might be supervising know that they're there; they've worked for this company, and now they've moved up.

There are opportunities to grow. If someone goes the extra mile, they might be the Star-of-the-Cruise or Employee-of-the-Month. If we see somebody that was doing something that wasn't their job and wasn't interested in moving up the ladder, then we see if we can recognize them some other way.

CHAPTER ELEVEN

❦ *Shoreside CPS Manager: Sharon Brown, U.K.*

I get them on board

Sharon works in the London office and helps cruisers simplify the process of emarking, with transfer service y coach or taxi from home to ship, and she keeps many records that knit together elements essential to a smooth operation at the port of emarkation and dearkation.

Connections with the seafarer's association help with issues involving the needs of the crew, and how they connect with their first assignment aoard ship. They are running a small café and a place where crew can go in and uy phone cards, toiletries and crisps. The Sea Chaplains are now allowed to come aoard.

It is important for the new crew to know there is someone

Sharon guides you to the ship

who will look after them oth efore an after oar in the ship.

I rememer last year , we had a group of 18 joining in Bristol, which is a kind of empty shell of a place. The Seafarers came over and took them for tea to help them out. Our port agents do that as well, if they know they will e there a long time. They will or anize foo an rinks for crew. Some of the crew have never een outsi e their own country efore.   When they get here, it is so regimented, ut it has to e or it would never work.

A lot of the crew see me on shore ecause I come to all the sailings. One of the restaurant waiters has worked here nine years, like myself, and he is always making me paper flowers. **The crew is like family, as they move from ship to ship workin .**

All of our ookings go into a data system , and I run all the reports, like how many passengers are joining, if they have a irthday, a special request, all the insurance documents, or a medical condition which we pass on to the doctor on oard .

> *I don't remember my room number, but could you tell me where my state room is?*

I make arrangements for the timing to oard. I know it will take aout three hours to disemark everyone. We like to start emarkation at least an hour efore dinner starts. That's a it of a tight frame ecause they have to do a muster drill efore dinner.

I also coordinate with the port how many people are coming, how many need to park cars, and how many coaches are arriving and leaving. Any special orders from the home office in Greece, like uniform accessories, have to come aoard as well.

After all the entertainers and craft instructors have received their contracts, then the room numers are assigned , and this is done for all the ships.

As Sharon says, I get them on oard!

CHAPTER TWELVE

Deck Storekeeper: Fadli: Indonesia

I follow the R.I.T.E. way [Respect, Integrity, Trust, and Excellence]

Where did I leave that wrench! Someone has to know where everything is! Our mothers aren't there to remind us where we set it down, so there has to e a system. Fortunately, there is one on the Columus, and Fadli plays the "Mom role" for the ship.

Fadli comes from the Barru region, located almost 100 km away from Makassar, the capital of South Sulawesi Province, in Indonesia. It's a place where the most eautiful utterflies in the world live. Sumatra is his home now, with hundreds of native languages, ut Indonesian is the main one. Fadli is head of the Indonesian community aoard the ship , meaning when it comes time to share special foods from his country, he makes the read!

"Tell us aout your jo?"

For four years now, Fa li says, the ship ecame my

Fadli: Motivated by organization

secon family. I am the Deck Storekeeper, ut also , I am multi-purpose, like the Captain's secretary, Staff Captain's secretary, and keeping the inventory of the deck department. We have three departments which are the Hotel Cost Controller, Engine, and Deck Storekeepers, who keep track of their own needs. Keeping track of paint used and mooring operations are my jo as well. In 2015 I left another company and now feel that this ship is my home. The crew and the passengers are all so very friendly, and it's not only from their words ut from their heart.

, You like learnin ao ut all the tra itions of the many nationalities on oar ¡ "

Like in Bali, they have the kecak ance, so we like sharin that ance, maye in the crew talent show . The Day of Silence, ack in Bali , is calle Nyepi which is a Hin u celeration. For 24 hours the people oserve total silence. The streets, an even the airport, are close . The women cook for ays in preparation of not havin any li hts on, usin the stoves for cookin , or makin noise. The ni ht efore is the o oh -o oh para e whose purpose is to purify the natural environment of any spiritual pollutants. When people visit Fadli from the cruise ship, he feels like they are part of his family and warns them that the local food is very spicy.

"Do you get out of your office and meet with passengers?"

Of course, when I am working around the ship, I stop and say hello and how are you.

"What is the most fun task you do in your jo?"

Inventory. It's like exercise to my rain ecause I have to rememer. By eing careful, I can save the company money y udgeting.

> It is a common superstition that it is unlucky to bring flowers aboard a cruise ship.
> Alternatively, it is considered good luck to spill wine on the deck.

"Are there differences etween working in a land jo compared to a sea jo?"

On a ship, every day I go outside my office, and there are so many people and crew to make me happy. In a land jo , I would work in an office in a small space. But on sea, there are so many cultures as well.

CHAPTER THIRTEEN

🦅 *Housekeeping Manager: Gabriel Matel: Romania*

Enjoy the free time

Think of your home, and the effort to keep it clean and neat. Now add 775 edrooms/aths and consider the size of the task!

"What su areas do you supervise or are responsile for , like the hand ironing or the ig man gle?"

The laundry. It's under my supervision. The launderettes on decks six and ten and also, the pulic areas like all the pulic toilets around , ut not inside the ars which is the ar department.

The cain stewards? Yes, 775 cains. So, our department is responsile for all the corridors, cains, and pulic toilets, crew cains etc. The crew have to clean their ca ins y themselves , ut the officer staff cains are my responsiility.

We have staff stewards for the staff and officers.

"The crew always look so neat and clean in their uniforms."

Our crew has two or three sets of uniforms. They wear one set for one day and then send to laundry and wear the second set the next day. Guests can send clothes to the laundry, and the next

Gabriel (HK), friends with Elvis (Bar)

day, in 24 hours, they will get it ack clean and folded. The laundry is taking care of crew and passengers as well. It's working 24 hours a day.

"Do you have a fact sheet on what you do?"

We wash 6,000 ed sheets , 6,000 pillowcases, and 6000 towels a week. Every day, we're using eight tons of water.

For driers, we have five, and for washers, we have four, of which one holds 85 kilograms. All linens, like the pillowcases, have to e pressed on the mangle. Last week the laundry received fifty of the magic ags , which are the ags we give to each passenger room to fill for a one price laundry special. Each item's lael has to e checked for requirement s of washing instructions.

"What is your life when you are not aoard ship?"

Two months with my family. Seven months on the ships. It's a funny thing: I've traveled almost all around the world, ut I never traveled in my country.

There are some places which I haven't seen. I want to do that. I'm looking forward. This time it will e summer , so I have planned a trip to the seaside. It will e my son's first time to the sea and to play in the sand. That is why I am here, for him and my family.

"If you were to advise a recruit that just came aoard, what would e the things that you would tell them to concentrate on?"

In the first month, I was taught to e strong, ecause you're going to hear a lot of things from different persons. He or she doesn't have to listen to what other persons are talking aout; they should get advice from the supervisor or department head.

The first month is hard, so don't listen to others whom you don't know.

Talk to the supervisor, and also, enjoy the free time.

Gabriel at work

"Most of the people that come into your department: are they new, or do they have to have some training in housekeeping or hotel?"

People just joining the ship have on-the-jo training the same day in the housekeeping department, like how to use the chemicals and how to act on oard . We have weekly scheduled training for all HK crew memers for laundry, room service, staff stewards and house cleaning.

The mangle presses linens

"So, where did you start?"

In 1999, I started as a galley utility. So that's really the ottom. I worked eight years for another company, and then I had a reak in 2007. I left that company. I went to England for aout seven months and worked in Newcastle and Witley Bay. In 2013 I talke to a frien ; we rew up to ether. He was workin with the CMV, an I aske him if he can put me in contact with the a ency. Employee recruitin ι[I starte a ain in 2013 when I joine the ship as a cain stewar . Step y step, year y year, I went up on the la er.

"What do you think motivated you to move up so fast?"

I liked the jo, and I like housekeeping items. I worked in reception and emarkation ut   wasn't really happy.

"Do you recommend that people try and find the jo that really suits them?"

Eight tons of water used every day

If they don't like, just a little it , the jo will not e done properly.
They will not do it right. It doesn't matter what kind of jo it is. I was   a cain
steward, and I liked cleaning, and actually, I was very proud of my eds . It
was like a spot on my rain that every ed was perfect. When you enter a
room it's the first impression, and I enjoyed it. I didn't expect promotion to e
so fast to e head of a department, ecause two years ago, I was just a night

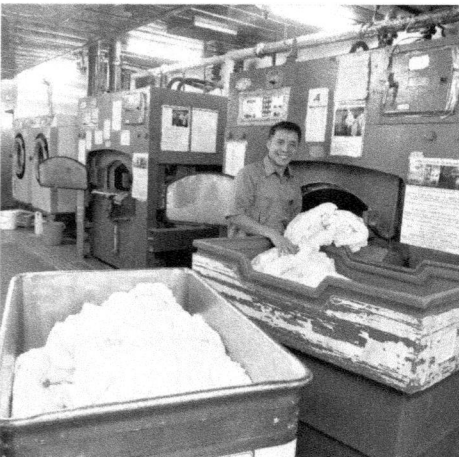

supervisor at the time. They called me
and said I had to replace the Chief
Housekeeper on Magellan. I said, who,
me?

We wash 6000 towels a week

CHAPTER FOURTEEN

🎁 *Restaurant Manager: Matthias Dobrzinski: Germany*

Welcome to my family

Matthias Dorzinski is from a small town near Frankfurt, Germany, and learned the restaurant usiness from his family's hotel , where he worked as a cook. He wished to have more contact with customers, so he migrated to the Dining Room, and the rest is history. He joined GCCL in 2006 and worked on river cruises ut wished to see more of the world, and then he egan with ocean ships, eventually leading to his work with CMV. He has lived in Colomia for several years and is proud to claim responsiility for putting together the restaurant team aoard the Columus.

He seems to e everywhere with his smile an an eye for supervision. His messa e for new people is: Welcome to my family. I am not only a restaurant oss; I am as well a person who listens to prolems an tries to solve them an help. You will learn all you nee to know step y step. Mistakes are no prolem , if you take them to learn.

Matthias has a table just for you

CHAPTER FIFTEEN

Bar Manager: Elvis Asan: Romania

If you give, it all takes place naturally

Every person alive will cheer for the individual who rises from modest eginnings to a major management position. Here is the story. Elvis rose to positions he never dreamed of. We paraphrase his comments which should give hope to anyone joining the CMV team.

I'm a ar manager, my second time on Columus. I started working with the crews in 2010. What I was doing then was cleaning in the galley. Then in two and a half months from my contract, I was promoted from utility cleaner to third cook. Before that, in the summer, I worked as a waiter. Then, I decided that I should start my career on cruise ships. That's how I ended up in 2010 with the cleaner jo. I egan y cooking food for the crew memers, and then to the main galley where I used to do cold appetizers, the artistic things that we love. Eventually, I moved over to the ar areas and learned aout eing a artender. Then , in the same contract, I moved up from crew ar artender. In 2012, I went ack on Marco Polo as assistant to the artender. My evaluation move me up one more step to arten er. For two years in a row I worke as arten er an then move up to assistant ar mana er, then ar mana er. I move very fast up the la er. I'm quite lucky.

A bar manager's favorite pastime

I am from Constanza, Romania, near the Black Sea. We have everything there. Mountain resorts and sea resorts. There are may e 40 or 50 Roma nians working on the ship now.

"Being a artender, do you have to have some kind of sparkle with people?"

What happened to me started when I was a student. I studied Economic Engineering Construction, so I could uild. Then I realized, me sitting in an office is not something I want to do for the rest of my life. Working as a waiter that first summer made me realize working with people was exactly what I wanted to do, not sitting and

> Every year, the average commercial cruise ship covers some 84,007 miles.

working with the numers , which is exactly what I am doing now. They say if you are trying to escape from something you don't like, you will end up doing it someday. I do love udgets. Even when I am home, I am working trying to find the easier way to improving my jo and what is related to those working under me to get things done, without forcing.

"Do you encourage your crew to e super friendly with the passengers?"

It's not encouraging them, its suggesting. I elieve that hospitality is somethin that only you, as a frien ly person, can o. I elieve that if you on"t like what you are oin , you ha etter fin somethin else.

So instead of forcing yourself to do something which you don't like, and then to feel, let's say, unhappy every day, it's etter to try to avoid it , or at least to try to understand what you can do to like it. Most of us here started in hospitality. It's of course difficult to work with people. It's very difficult. No matter.

We nee to have that pleasure to say, yes, I"m oin to work. It"s attitu e for those thin s, isn"t it; Goo attitu e. If you ive, it all takes place naturally.

One of the interesting things that I do is correspond with former guests. I like to have a lot of friends. Then I started to have friends in ports. I'm still keeping in touch.

Funny stories? There are a lot of them. I like to live in the present, and what was in the past, it stays in the past. You don't retain those things. Also, when I finish a contract, when I step out from the ship, this life stays here, and then I go. When I get ack, I live in that world, two different lives.

"Is there any advice that you can give us to write aout for other crew memers?"

The same advice I give to myself, ecause it was quite difficult and tough at the very eginning. For me in that time , I was for the first time away from home. It was far away for me, ecause I had vacations with my friends, with my family to go to different places in Romania, ut not so far. If they want to uil a future an e as stron as possile, they nee to un erstan that everythin that they're oin , it's for themselves. I call workin on the ship a pai vacation, ecause you"re pai for what you are oin onoar . Then in the same time you have the opportunity of seein the worl . You are quite lucky, ecause there are passengers just spending a lot of money so they can see the world. It's a good experience. You can really like your work. I feel like a fish out of water. If I go ack ho me, and I would choose to stay and not work on a cruise ship, I would think it would e quite difficult.

Crew foosball tournament

"What, tasks do you like to do the most or are fun and that you really look forward to?"

Everything which keeps me usy. As long as I am usy   , I do like challenges. It is aout trying to understand the crew and also aout eing fair with them. For me, everyody's the same, no matter the color of the skin, or nationality. No matter if I just met you or knew you for a long time. As a manager, I like to e as fair as possile. I'm a strict manager   , this is true. But in the same time, I like to e as fair as possile.

"Do you ever feel that a guest might've come ack , partly, ecause you made friends with them? You have to e proud of that."

I do have guests during the world cruise, who told me that they chose for that reason, so it makes you feel good. I'm a proud person. Maye sometimes I'm showing too much, ut I feel like when you see the   uests enjoyin themselves, it's a oo feelin when you et oo comments re ar in your crew memers. It makes you feel prou   that you are oin your jo.

CHAPTER SIXTEEN

🦅 *Shore Excursion Manager: Ediie Abliakimova: Crimea*

It's boring without challenges

Cruise ships are the entertainers of the ocean that offer everything from live musicians to sunathing. But in addition to keeping passengers happy day and night while at sea, they have a shore excursion team who works to expose the passengers to the sights and sounds after arriving into each port.

"What are your position and duties?"

I organize and promote excursions. We communicate everything

> Do I have to go to the mandatory boat drill?

with the local suppliers and supervise the smooth running of the excursions and the whole operation.

"Do you have any comments with respect to the multi-cultural situation with passengers? Are there challenges ecause of the different languages or customs?"

The excursion clients come from ifferent cultures an are ifferent types of people as well. They have ifferent min sets an mentalities. A guide may need to have a different approach to them, ut generally most on the Columus are British people. We are quite used t o working with British people. Sometimes there are challenges. Things don't exactly follow the general plan, ecause everything is suject to conditions. It epen s on the weather an thin s, ut enerally it is a oo customer relationship with the passen ers we have.

"Do you feel the enrichment that we are giving to people is one of the main reasons that they like coming on the cruises?"

Yes, people come on cruises, and especially on world cruises, to see places and learn aout them. When they go on excursions, they have an opportunity to see and to learn and experience the highlights of the places spread all over the itinerary. Those that go independently might know something in general, ut not exactly. Or maye they will get lost and waste time or miss the insights availale from the guides. By organizing and planning the excursions for them, we use the short time ashore efficiently.

"By using the guides, you are actually teaching the passengers something?"

The guides are all local, and some are native speakers who can give first-hand experiences as well. They share their culture and their stories aout themselves. So, you come into contact with a person who actually represents the country, who has good knowledge of the places, so yes, it is learning and enriching.

"Finding out aout the economics of a country helps one to understand what is going on?"

Yes, ut eing an educated person and eing interested in many things and reading many ooks , that is a totally different thing from experiencing it yourself. When you o to the country, an see how it is, feel the atmosphere an talk to the local people, that is ifferent from what you rea from the ooks. You et a new insi ht an etter un erstan in , which is a way to wi en your own knowle e experience. I think travelin , especially on the worl cruises, chan es the mentality of people.

We went to Papua New Guinea; a very poor country. Looking ack, we often complain aout our lives. It is human nature to say this is not perfect or that is not perfect or our positions are not good. But you see

Ediie organizing more excursions

the differences and see how these people live in totally different conditions, and you can't imagine how to even survive in those conditions. It changes

you and makes you appreciate things more or makes you have a different viewpoint.

"Does your staff put together the presentation?"

Yes, we do all the research ut also receive information from our local agents: from people who live in these countries. They share the images with us. They share their experience. Descriptions and explanations are a joint effort. Sometimes things change over time.

"What interaction do you have with the crew?"

The ship has ecome like a family. We have many ifferent nationalities in the crew, an

> *The HMS Black Joke was previously a Brazilian slave ship called the Henriquetta that was captured by the Royal Navy and repurposed to chase down slave ships, ultimately freeing hundreds of slaves during her five-year career.*

sometimes you have many people from your own country, ut often you on"t. It makes you like a family. You talk to them, eat with them, spen a lot of time with them. In fact, we spend with crew more time than we spend with our families.

It also helps you to understand the other people and maye some places where I've never een: to Myanmar for instance. Now I know many people from there. They tell aout the culture of their countries. You et to know how they are as well. You will see some typical features aout this nationality or another nationality. I think it's very enrichin .

"What aout your own country and growing up?"

I'm actually from Crimea. We have eaches, mountains, fores ts, and a lovely place to e. Every time I return, it's such a holiday for me to e there. Even though we have a very nice itinerary that's very interesting in diversity, the place where you're from is something special. It's family.

"Would you ever want to e a tour guide in Crimea?"

I see the difference of eing a guide and eing a manager for an organization. I think it's very interesting to e a guide, ecause you have so much knowledge, and you tell people aout this, you know, and so of course it's real interesting; I like what I'm doing.

It can e sometimes very tough, especially when we have many ports in a row, and sometimes you have several ports in one day, which happens as well. The jo is very intense. We don't have a fixed schedule , like you go to work at nine and end at five. Sometimes we have excursions scheduled in such a way that you have to e flexile all the time, and you have to e there all the time.

"When the last us comes into port, a caring shepherd, one of your people, is there to greet them?"

Sometimes the rides are in traffic; the plan to have four uses ack y seven o'clock surprises us when they return at nine. This is something affected y factors eyond our control   .

"How do you motivate yourself, eing   around strangers always, and you are always in their presence?"

I think it has to do with your inner happiness. I"m quite happy with my life. I"m happy with my family an   with my frien s. I"m happy with my relationships. I"m   enerally without much to complain aout; the jo can e stressful sometimes, ut it" s a part of it. Any jo woul   e stressful, an sometimes you have to   o thin s which you are not fon   aout or   on't want to   o.

But it's a positive. It's , take it or leave it". There are some thin s which are more   ifficult to   o, ut I like it just as well. I think it's orin   without challen es.

"It keeps you thinking and keeps you young?"

Indeed, it keeps you involved all the time. You have to look for different solutions. You have to learn a lot as well from different situations, from complicated ones especially. You have to do things which are not standard. Sometimes you make right decisions. Sometimes you make wrong ones; it's everywhere like this, ut you always learn.

Even a ad   experience rings something to the future for your own development. Next time you know how to deal with it. You're etter prepared. You have to face so many situations every day, and you learn how to deal with them.

"Have you made any close friends outside of your own culture?"

I have very good friends in India and

> We boarded a shuttle bus at one of the stops to take us into town. Soon after leaving the dock we passed a long, golden beach. A lady sitting behind me said 'Oh what a lovely beach. I didn't realize we would be so near the sea.

in Romania. Romania is very close to my country so their mindset may e similar, ut   India is very far away, a different mentality. I also have good ones in China. All people are   ifferent, ut a t the same time, human nature is similar isn't it¡ It's interestin to have   ifferent connections an to learn   ifferent cultures an to have frien s in   ifferent parts of the worl .

But I think at the same time, you nee to make an effort for this as well. You nee to compromise, an many thin s require us to e open min e , ecause what is accepta le in some countries may e unaccepta le in others.

I have to respect this. Whenever you go to a different country or face a different culture and people, you have to respect their rules. Accept them, rather than rin in your own worl to them while tryin to promote it. That takes an effort as well.

Expressed another way, you're our est travel witness that we've had, so share your worldly acceptance with all around you. You're very much in control of your thou hts an lo ic. The worl appreciates that.

Entertainment team at the Great Wall of China

Ready to climb the Great Wall of China

CHAPTER SEVENTEEN

🌺 *Hotel Cost Controller: Lipson Fernandez: India*

Predicting a need for eggs

Of course, someone needs to count the eggs! Each crew memer should appreciate the importance of a cost controller's work. The usiness would e inefficient without cost control, and inefficient usinesses do not survive, causing jo loss.

"What kind of work do you do on Columus?"

My jo is in regard to whatever food and everages we have on oard. I'm the one who orders those things and sends the orders to the supply department shoreside. Then they send to the different suppliers, and then we get the products. We have certain time frames, like schedules, to ring

Lipson checking on food storage

the things in on oard the ship, and this is how we schedule the loadings.

The reports have everything: the time, date, everything is there. How many days it will last?

These are all the suppliers. Beverage, food and hotel and my charts show all the suppliers. You try to control all of these files. So, you trust all the suppliers to e on time with the goods.

"Does it ever happen that they don't show up or don't have enough products or they misunderstand the order?"

My jo is to go through all the orders , and then I send to shoreside and they are the ones to deal with all the suppliers. Others deal with quality and issues that arise during the cruise.

In case, if I see some ad quality, I make a report. We have a special report with the photos in it, and then I send it to the supply department. Then they do all these discrepancy items.

"How long have you een doing this particular jo?"

I've een doing this jo for twenty years. I'm now forty-three, ut I look very young, people tell me. For CMV, it is only ten years now I have een working.

"You monitor how many potatoes people eat?"

In one day, we use 345 Kilos of potatoes. Yes. I am the one who does all the orders and checks them, ecause some supplies have to e ordered two months in advance. We have to focus on the forward requirements. We have to support the future.

"So, the chef has to report these needs?"

Hotel cost controller

The Chef doesn't do any ordering. He only takes what he needs. If reserves are needed, he makes that cushion. I'm the one also who handles other items like cleaning supplies, so all of those things are there.

Ideally, I keep track of what is moving on a daily asis. For example, for 30 days, you can predict a need for eggs. Total is 67,000 eggs.

I keep track of each and every item. How it's moving. Each department, like the Chef or the Bar Manager, gives me their requisitions.

Why is a safety drill called a muster?
Muster simply means to gather.

We have storekeepers for meat, fresh foods, vegetales , etc. The paperwork from the requisitions goes to the storekeeper, and if there are changes, like in kilos, those changes are noted.

"So, the requisition is really the thing that starts the all rolling."

Yes, and every evening I see stock on hand, how it is moving, everything's moving. Then we come to know exactly how it moved.

I do a lot of other things. A lot of things are already starting to come for May, which is three months away.

"How long does something stay frozen? A couple of years?"

Yes, ut it moves y its dates. We watch the prices   , like something might e one euro here and six euros in Asia.

"How many people work under you?"

We have a total of 11 people under me.

"Do you have a container ship that's coming with some food?"

We had some containers in Sydney. Now we have containers coming in Singapore with dry stores. It all depends on the temperature also.

"How many nationalities do you have in your team?"

Only a few, ecause we are a small group , ut we work very well together. I give them free time when I can, ecause we don't have Saturday and Sunday off.

When the crew come in as new, they start in storage utility. My people, if they are happy enough, if they want to grow, then we give them promotions. If they do a good jo, then they change. They go somewh ere maye in different departments.

"What is consumed the most on the ship?"

The daily moving is eggs, flour, sugar, potatoes, carrots. The average amount of potatoes used in one day is 345 kilos or 9200 kilos in a month. All the preparation is done down here. We have sections for all the meat, fish and vegetales. It is cut down here and then moved to the main galley.

We have a procedure for everything like cutting carrots. There is a log of when it was taken out of the store, how long it was stored, and when it was taken up to the galley. Everything is logged in, ecause sometimes we have inspections coming on oard the ship. They check on these things.

"How do you keep your milk fresh or do you use powdered milk?"

We uy milk in cartons and use y the date on carton , and it doesn't have to e refrigerated. Some we keep in the daily stores.

"Okay, so how much eer is consumed in a day or a month or a week?"

It depends, ecause if we have certain nationalities, then we have a dark eer.   In checking one rand, we used 180 cans in one day. For a month we used 15,300 of ottles and cans of eer.   I also order linen and uniforms.

"So how do you know when to order new sheets and towels?"

I can see the stock. Also, I ask the Chief Housekeeper.

"What do you like aout your jo?"

I like my jo very much , and I like the figures to work with and all the charts. I like gadgets and play music. I played for the crew talent show. I love the music.

I started guitar when I was six years old. I like all parts of my jo, and ecause of these figures, I like the jo very well.

, How o you know in the first place how to uy for a Worl Cruise¡ "

Experience counts a lot. Sometimes we have to   uess. For example, in Europe, sometimes we have more Scottish or Irish. We have to know what kin of eer the Irish like. Maye t he previous cruise was all English, and they don't like to drink Guinness Beer. Then I have to ask myself, which nationalities will e on oard   , and what do they like to drink.

, What aout foo . Different cultures like to eat ifferent kin s of foo ¡ "

Meat is meat ut fixe in ifferent styles , with a variety of spices.

"If you find your storage of potatoes or carrots is getting way too ig, do you tell the Chef to start pushing those items?"

No, it's never like that. Some things, like onions, we can keep outside, and we just order less on the next order. In Japan the price of onions was very high, so we ordered extra onions efore going there and just kept them, and that is how we play with things and save the company money. It makes a ig differ ence.

CHAPTER EIGHTEEN

🎁 *Duty-Free Manager: Carolina Topalov: Romania*

Every day we learn something

Cruise ships have an on-board shopping mall with a boutique selling handbags and cruise clothing, a high-end jewelry store, and the most visited store selling duty-free items like perfume and, of course, chocolates.

"What do you do as the Manager of the shops?"

I am responsible to hold our team together and to give the best service to our customers. I'm head of the team.

"Do you choose the items in your shops or is that done by the land company, and do you do the inventory also?"

Some of the items, yes. We do the inventory as we need the stock control.

"What things sell best in the shop?"

That is chocolate! Nobody can live without their chocolate! No matter what, even if the food is excellent, people everywhere need their chocolate.

| What time is the midnight buffet? |

"Do you think there are advantages to cultural diversity on board the ship?"

That is true from so many points. For me as a person, I'm experienced, and can meet so many people from different countries; even for the guests, it's interesting. When you have time, and you interact with the crew, they tell you their stories, the tradition in their country, and their way about the food. We do share all this information. We are curious.

We ask questions. We ask each other if we have the same type of food, because it looks the same. It's a good experience. Yes, it is true. We are from all over the world, and every country has their own habits. And gestures. I used to work with Italians. They use more of the hands. Some of the crew are more hugging. Some people don't have this in their culture. Some cultures don't want you to stand too close. Latino people are very friendly, very warm. They are touching and hugging. Nordics are not that way, but that doesn't mean that they're not friendly. They're not used to being so warm. I worked with Polish people, and they were very cool. But, when you talk, you realize that actually they are not. They don't express like us that much.

"How do you break the ice and start talking with someone?"

I know it comes naturally. I don't know. I will just go. I don't think that I will disturb them. I think when we start to have a conversation, it will be natural; I don't just go and ask or say hello. There comes a moment when you may sit at the same place, and you start to talk.

"What motivates you or makes you shine?"

Shop manager

I think the main reason is it's because you are traveling, and if you like the world, that's a very positive thing. The next thing you know, you are in the next port. If you are working in a happy environment, we are a family here. When you go on vacation, and then you come back to the same people, you are so happy. Like it's your brother, and here I am, I am back.

"What do you miss from the ship when you are home?"

Depends on how long you are home. If you stay longer, you might miss the ship.

"Because you are involved with the ship, what has been successful to get people to come in and purchase things?"

I think it's always interacting with our guests. Not only for the main goal, which is to buy. First, we do the interaction. This is our main goal; everybody should buy. It's not the same on land. People come and go, and you never know when you will see them again. But you see people often here; even on a seven-day cruise, you have a chance to see people almost every day.

"How many people are employed in the shops?"

Six people, and we are very close.

"What advice do you have for everyone in getting along with different cultures?"

The crew on board are very nice, and they know what it means when someone new comes on board. We know how he feels, and we are going to be the ones to interact with him. We see that look. You forget where your cabin is, or where you need to go. No need to give them advice, because crew will always do the right thing.

"What do you think you have learned from working on the ship?"

Being organized. Timing. To do the things in the certain amount of time you have. When you go back home, you are quick to get things done. When you go shopping, in half an hour, it's all done. It's like a school here, you don't realize you are gaining skills.

"Relationship skills are gained working with strangers?"

We don't feel it that way. It's like, when you are home, and you have new people coming over, we feel the same here, like its new friends coming in.

"Is there something you have done before that you continue to do that has worked well for training?"

Honestly, my opinion is every day we learn something. Every day we make mistakes, and we learn from those mistakes. You just feel what is right.

"What do you like best about your job?"

Every day means customer service and working with people. I didn't know in the beginning that I could do this kind of job. I started as a cabin steward. Slowly I moved up, and you grow and develop skills you didn't know you had along the way. It's like you grow up here.

Tidying the store

"Did you have a role model while you were a cabin steward?"

I think it goes back to how you are raised. I took each day as it went, and if I am able to do this, then fine and if not, fine. The moment I can feel I can do more, then I will try.

"Where would you like to be in five years?"

I've been working on ships for fifteen years, and I would like to still be here in the same job. I like working on the sea, and going on land feels a little strange, but we can switch quickly. Most of my family are working on ships. My dad was a Captain, so maybe he was my role model for getting a ship job. There are six brothers and sisters, so it is a big family.

CHAPTER NINETEEN

🎗 *IT Manager: Vladimir Jovanovic: Serbia*

Use the resource carefully

Computers. Wi-Fi. The web. How did we live without them? These workers handle all IT matters for the ship, including a satellite service that connects the ship to the internet via a rental of the resources that can be shared among the guests and crew members. The more people that access the internet satellite connection at the same hour, the slower the resource will be. But it has a heavy cost to the ship per month, thousands of pounds or dollars, and people need to adapt by seeking access during low-use periods. The best times are late at night or early morning.

The charge is not made according to minutes used, but rather data uploaded or downloaded, and the person renting the resource buys the amount needed; that usage is conveyed when the person signs on and off.

These experts suggest to crew members that they use the resource carefully, both as to time and cost. The time will be efficient

I.T. Manager

during late night hours, and the cost will be less when sending a simple email or text. The things to avoid would be video and any large portion of bytes of data.

Vladimir likes working with people, so that is the main opportunity.

"How do new people coming aboard deal with communicating with their family?"

The biggest issue on every ship is that most people are used to a much better quality of internet. We have smaller band widths, and people use their devices to the maximum. If I want to send a video call or watch YouTube on the ship, that is nearly impossible. I tell the new crew coming on board to use internet, but only use Viber, WhatsApp, or send an email.

Use texting and emails, especially during off hours when others are not using it. For passengers the best time is between 2:00pm and 4:00pm when most of the crew are resting and not using Wi-Fi.

When new crew are embarking right away on the gangway, I meet with them and say, first, before you buy internet, come talk with me about the best ways to use the Wi-Fi. One thing I've learned is that I feel very needed here. This is one of the most essential services the ship offers.

For a new crew member, the option to communicate with family and friends at home is a welcome resource to assure that all is well, even on the high seas. Many people have found that for large chunks of data, stopping in port in a place with free Wi-Fi is a prudent way to save on internet costs.

CHAPTER TWENTY

Dancer: Hollie Glossop: UK

We are all in the same boat

Guests love to e entertained. Production numers with color and glitter , lovely gals and guys, great music, and incredile dance choreography are availale just for walking a few paces from cain to show. There are other acts as well, ut the production numers on the Columus are not to e missed.

"Why did you choose a sea jo?"

I always wanted to work on cruise ships since I started dancing. And there are not that many dancing jos on land, unless you go into the West End

Holly Dancing

or something like that, where you need to sing as well. And I don't sing.

Cruise ship dance companies are the first place that you look for a contract. This is my fourth contract, and I have een head dancer efore. The current

Dance Captain has done several world cruises and has worked for the cruise line for ten years. I am the only En lish ancer, so all the rest are Ukrainian or from Belarus, so they all speak Russian.

They have helped me a lot, ecause they have to translate everything for me. I know the key words, and I can react to them. I know when she said start from the eginning , or use your right arm or your left leg, ut I don't speak Russian.

I was one of the only English-ased people at the eginning of my friend, Craig's, contract. I helped him a lot, and he said I was the reason he decided to stay.

We all have to help each other, ecause we are all in t he same oat ¥[an everyone ets a little it homesick sometimes an are worrie that they can"t o somethin .

Since we've all "een there", everyone knows what to say to cheer the other one up. I rememer , when I first arrived, they showed me to my cain. I had traveled all night. I was really tired, and I looked at the cain . I could feel myself tearing up, ecause I really didn't know what I was doing. What did I let myself in for? Then, maye two hours a fter that, I met my really good friend who was a dancer on another ship. She came one month efore me , ut she knew where to go and what to do, and it made me feel so much at ease and happier.

It helps if you've got someone as a friend to show you what to do.

"Did your attitude aout cultures change when you got on the ship , ecause you were not used to e ing around such a variety of cultures?"

I never met people from so many nationalities, so you just on't really think aout it. It's opene my eyes to lo ts of new cultures. Everyone ets on so well. We're all so ifferent, an there are never any prolems. Most people speak a oo level of En lish, so we can all communicate well.

"What's the strangest experience you've had since you've een here?"

I'm really ad for my wardroe malfunctions on stage. Even on this cruise, during the Fiesta Show, my fake hair piece fell out, and my skirt was undone. On my first contract, we did the ABBA Show where we wear the ig show girly skirts, and I rememer I went to put my foot down ehind, and my heel got stuck in the dress. I landed on my ack; I was like a turtle. If that happened to me now, I'd e laughing.

"What interests you aout your jo? Why dancin   g?"
I've always wanted to dance. Always. I started when I was two and a half, so that's all I've ever known. It's kind of hard to stop now, to go ack to England and get a normal jo. Seems so izarre. Like I don't know what it would e like to wake up in the same place every day and do the same jo every single day.

"What do you think you have learned from working on a cruise ship?"

From four years a o, I've efinitely ecome more confi ent as a person, ecause you have to talk to passen ers all the time. Proaly, if you aske me to o this on my first contracts, I ha to e a it nervous. I really wouldn't know what to say. Now, we just talk to everyone all the time.

"Is it hard to always e smiling and on your est ehavior in front of guests?"

No not really. Even if you are in a ad mood , you always want to smile.

People love the shows. People just compliment all the time. How would we not like that?

"What motivates you to do your est work?"

To do the show, I don't know if it's all my dancer training. If you ever go on the stage, you have to give it 100%. It'd e izarre now to go on to do a show and not try your est.

"If you were to advise someody just coming on, what would you say?"

> If the ship sinks, I hope there are ice cream machines on the lifeboats.

For new crewmemers, I" say just e nice to everyo y. I just sm ile an say hello to everyo y, ecause when you first o on, you on"t know who anyone is. The est thing, if you're nice to everyone, then sometimes you know a ar man might get you a drink quicker or, in the galley, they might e ale to give you some nice food or whatever. If you're nice to everyone, then everyone's going to e nice ack to you, aren't they?

"Have you had to face emergencies or difficult situations?"

No. Someody had a fall ecause of a ig wave. The show was aout to egin , so we just kept the lights on till they were helped. Nothing scary, though.

"Do you think you have a secret in getting along with people? Is it your personality or from eing around everyone else?"

Yes, I think in the entertainment world we are all friends, like a family. We don't really have a choice, since we are together all the time. So, you are going to ecome really good friends. We are all like-minded. We all know what it's aout.

"Are there customs aout others that you find interesting? "

One weird thing in England, when it's your irthday it's a custom when you go out that your friends uy you a drink. With the Ukraine crew, on their irthday , they uy everything. So, they go to the crew ar four nights efore and uy all the drinks in advance. It 's hard to get used to that.

Holly winning at Bingo

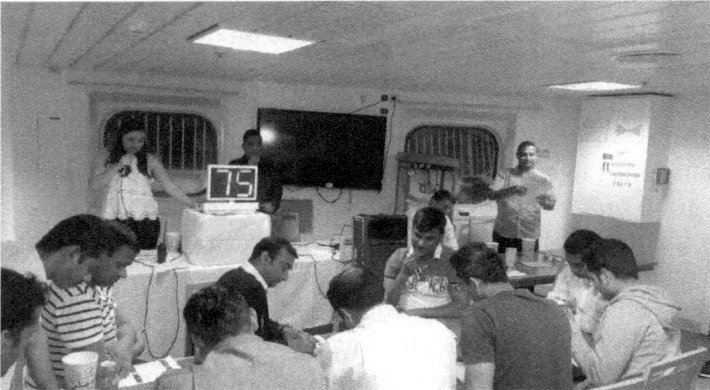

Bingo prize is 1000 British pounds

" , What are ifferent customs of the Ukrainians that you are not use to¡
They like to keep to themselves an uil a arrier , ut once you reak
own that arrier, they are amazin .

CHAPTER TWENTY-ONE

🎁 *Band-Drums: Craig Gilbraith: UK*

It's nice to have some fresh challenges

It's good for crew and guest alike to e aware that the ship has its own and and that it plays   everything from show tunes to operatic numers. There is no and without a drummer to set the eat. We can listen to a first   -hand account from that drummer in the summary elow.

"Why did you want a sea jo?"

I was never looking to do a professional jo ; it was always more of a hoy. And when the opportunity to play the drums full time on a ship came along, I took to it straight away.

Going around the world while playing an instrument is just an asolute dream come true. It's not every day you get this opportunity to e literally on the other side of the world. The places I'd never dreamed of. I never even heard of them. It turns out to e great, like for example, we had a great day in Guatemala and in places I never would go to; then I get to play the drums as well.

"This is a high-pressure jo with lots of energy. Do you like that?"

Craig during rehearsal

I thrive on that. I need to e usy. It's nice to have some fresh challenges, and to do something completely different.

This is my first contract, so I have een on oard three months now. So far so good. I could see myself doing three, four contracts. Just continue on with it eing my career for the next few years.

, Which of the cultures or nationalities o you seem to   et alon   with¡ "

I like the Ukrainians with the an , an there's one uy in the an from the Philippines. The lan ua e arrier is really ifficult. We somehow mana e, an it all comes to ether an soun s incre ile. When you reak it own, the uitarist an myself can't communicate in lan ua es. I can't speak Russian, an he can't speak much En lish.

We can just sit own, put out the music that I woul play, an it soun s amazin . Which is quite something really. I feel like that we just speak through the music.

"Does someone in Greece arrange for all the music and parts and all?"

We have a andleader who copies and compiles everything. We learn our its individually, and then we ring it all together; they make a few amendments, and that is how it works.

"What do you think motivates you to do your est?"

I think this is one of the most difficult things I've done, eing so far away from home. Yes, I played the drums efore, ut nothing on this professional scale. It's completely different, and I just want to e the est I can e; it was my hoy, ut now it's my jo, ut it's still my hoy. I'm still lo ving it, and I just want to ecome a etter drummer.

I want to ecome a etter person, and this is definitely doing that. Like how hard and difficult things are. The shows, and this jo, have made me work so much. And it's made me so much etter. I come f rom a very small town near Newcastle. Not a very wealthy area. There are not any musical opportunities unless you go to London. Which is 5 hours away. Which is why this opportunity makes me want to e the very est I can e.

"And do you like the food?"

I am a fussy eater, ut there is always food to eat , three meals a day, plus a midnight uffet. I always find something I like , ut I stick to pastas and stay away from the curries and fish.

"When you came aoard , was there someone kind of like a uddy to tak e you around?"

No, until I found Hollie, the dancer. There were 12 British on oard. If someone comes on oard in the middle of a cruise , then the Crew Amassador

Iain, Holly, Craig, and Lee being interviewed

would help you. But if you come aoard while the ship is in dry dock at the very eginning , then noody is really ready for you , as there is a lot of cleaning and maintenance going on.

But it was really difficult, ecause I am not trained in the technical stuff , and here was this and who all spoke Russian. I met Hollie , and she took me under her wing and helped me through the first three weeks. Suddenly, like overnight, everything seemed to fit in place. I started making friends, and now I don't spend any time in the cain , as I am always out doing things.

"Did your attitude change aout other cultures when you came aoard?"

Yes, in my culture, everyone expects everyone to speak English, which is really ad of us. I t's a weird thing, ecause I really like languages , ut yet I haven't learned any. It's made me really appreciate other cultures.

You see all these ifferent cultures, an it is amazin . Everyone just works for one i team. I just smile to them, an they'll smile ack, an everyone's a i family. Everyone ets on really well.

, Are there customs of other cultures that you fin ifficult to eal with, or really interestin ¡"

With the an , they are kin of strict, like everythin is lack an white. I coul have a eate with someone for an hour , an they woul just say, no, it's this way or that. It's not a a thin , just interestin . I sit there in and rehearsal and try to understand what's going on. The way they say words, it's totally different.

"What motivates you to work when you are really exhausted? How do you find the energy to get up and go?"

Proaly looking at the map and seeing where I am going to e in the next few weeks. That's the motivation in the grand scheme of things. I want to see the ports as much as the passengers. I just want to do my jo as est as I can   , so I can see the ports and have a good time.

CHAPTER TWENTY-TWO

✿ *Keyboard-band: Anastasia Suhodolskaia: Moldova*

Music is the best language

What is a and without a talented keyoard musician? Anastasia is an example of the challenges that languages present to people willing to e accepting friends. The aility to communicate is a major help to relationships. Fortunately, she has the universal language of music to ring her friends together.

"Tell us a little it aout how you got here and what you do?"

My position is show-an musician, an every ay I have a rehearsal. There are six of us in the show and. We listen to the audio and then have to write sheet music. We have the trumpet player from Moldova, who is my rother, the ass player, who is the and leader from Ukraine, the guitar player from Ukraine, Craig the drummer from England, and the saxophone player from the Philippines. We try to understand, ecause it's a little it confusing when we play. Where do we start, and what do we play? It is not easy, ecause of the ifferent nationalities an languages.

Keyboard player Anastasia

lan ua es. But we like what we o, an it is a oo experience to o somethin to ether.

"What is the funniest thing that has happened to you when you used the wrong word to someone speaking a different language?

It is always funny, and we laugh all the time. My English is not so good, so we try. Craig speaks only English, so every time he jokes, ecause he doesn't understand what we say to him. We laugh and apologize.

"What would you advise someone new coming aoard the ship?"

I don't know ecause music is the est language.

, Do you ever talk aout customs at Christmas or New Years¡ "

Yes of course. We talk aout how we celerate. It's very interestin to learn aout another country.

"What motivates you to do your est jo?"

I really like this jo ecause I can travel. When I was in my country, I played in the music conservatory. I played in a ig jazz orchestra , and my salary was very small, ecause this was something new for my country, a jazz and. Noody wanted to pay for this type of music. Some musicians had

> In 2010, the aircraft carrier USS Carl Vinson was deployed to Haiti after the 2010 earthquake and provided the island with 200,000 gallons a day of fresh drinking water from its desalination plants.

worked on a ship and said you can try. I wanted the jo very much. I don't know how it happened, ut I sent a video to the Ukraine office, and they liked my video and hired me. I am so happy to e ale to see the world. In my country , I would never have een ale to go to Bora Bora, and when I went there, I said to myself, I can't elieve I am here.

"Do you think this will e your permanent career?"

It's really good for me for the experience. Plus, I can play my music, not just the show tunes, and I feel I can move up in my position.

"Have you made new friends here?"

Yes, of course. Now I have a lot of frien s across the loe. It's my secon contract, an I have a few frien s from my first contract year. One is Olga in the shop. Oh yes. She worked on Magellan also. And when we meet here, it's like a ig family, and all from CMV. We have friends everywhere. So, we can call and say hello.

"Do your Columus friends come from other countries too?"

Yes, of course. Olga from Ukraine. Usually it's from Ukraine or Belarus, you know, ut now we have friends from the Philippines; friends happen from England, like Craig.

"Woul you like to visit your frien 's country as well¡ "

Yes. Everyo y says come to my country. Especially in Ukraine, it's very easy. But my mother wants me to tell her everything. I come from a musical family. My father and mother are oth musicians. I am the oldest , and then one rother plays the trumpet , and the other plays the accordion, and two sisters are singers. My parents are very proud every time they call and talk with us.

Crew BBQ

, Do you like all the variety of cultures on oar , since it's so har to communicate with people¡"

It's ecause I think everyo y has a lot of time for un erstan in . Sometimes we just look at someody, and it's okay . I understand. We spend a lot of time together, and it's up to us.

"Cultures have different kinds of nonveral gestures and communication. Is that hard?"

Bar B Q

No, never does that happen. Everyody tries to understand. We don't have a prolem .

.

CHAPTER TWENTY-THREE

🌸 *Mykola Zubashevsky: Ukraine*

Dancing that comes from the soul

What does it take to e a dancer on a cruise ship? An advanced dance ackground and eing skilled at lots of different dance disciplines is the most important consideration to join a cruise ship's entertainment team. A dancer must also e friendly, profes sional with a good stage presence, not e shy to perform in pulic, e ready for anything like sudden ship

Mykola dancing in Fiesta show

movement, learn choreography quickly, and e on their toes --literally. Mykola, known as Nikoli y his friends , has mastered all the aove.

"As a dancer what are your responsiilities?"

I'm responsile for all movements on the stage, my costumes and rehearsals.

, Why i you choose a sea jo instea of workin on lan ¡ "

Because I like travel an the ship was a natural place.

"How long does it take to learn a whole new act?"

The show we are doing tonight is a new act, not for me, ut for some , and we all have to e together. To learn the new act takes a total of five days.

"I don't understand how you can learn that fast?"

Most companies you learn on land. Tonight, we are going to have this show and then forget this show and learn a new one, ecause we have three new shows till the end of this cruise.

"So, you completely forget?"

Not completely, ecause I dance this show on other ships. This is my sixth contract with CMV. But we have different steps,

> The replica of the 18th century rigger HMS Bounty which was built for the film "Mutiny on the Bounty," stayed afloat for over 4 decades before it sank when it was inexplicably sailed into the eye of Hurricane Sandy in 2012.

different counts for the same numer/song .

"What happens to the costumes you are using for tonight's show?"

Yes, the costumes are African, so after tonight we will wash them and put ack stage for the next year maye.

"I am curious as to how you can always e smiling when you are dancing. Do you just glue a smile in place?"

It's not like it's real, like from my soul, ecause I just can't dance with on ly a smile. When dancing, I just try to feel the music, all the steps to please the passengers. I love jumps and stretches.

"What motivates you to do this dancing that comes from the soul?"

When I give all my power for the passengers, I receive the applause and these emotions, they motivate me to do the next dance. If I don't have the power, I get on the stage and try to do more if I can.

"What does it feel like to e on the stage? Is it like a high that uilds your confidence?"

For the first time when we learn the show, for example, it's like you are nervous, you are excited, and you start with a new partner. But when you hear the first chord of music, you forget aout this , and you try to do all that you can.

"Is that hard to do to work with one girl, then another one?"

Sometimes yes, ecause , from the start, we are learning together, so we need time to try and feel the part.

CHAPTER TWENTY-FOUR

Housekeeping Jolly: Sean Gracias: India

My job is to make everyone happy

A "jolly" is a new word for most of us. To folks new to cruise ships, this summary y Sean , defining a "jolly", is helpful.

Helping Guests: Sean's passion

We make everyone happy, starting from emarkation; we welcome the passengers in. We help them out with the safe ox. We check out if there's any prolems in their cain. We see the advance copy note from the reception people and go to their cain personally with the message. We make sure they are satisfied in explaining what prolem they have. We tell the prolem to reception. So may e it can e solved immediately after that. We normally do the office work also, like take the things from one department here to the other for signatures: the hotel director to the captain, or we even take the letters from the reception to the captain and the passengers. We are asically the communication etween all the departments , so we can explain an issue to the passengers; we help if the passengers don't understand what the reception is saying, or if the reception doesn't understand what the passengers are saying; the passengers learn their prolem, and we explain it to the reception so they can have it fixed.

"Where did the word "jolly" come from?"

That is what they say or do on the radio. Whoever needs us calls on the radio with "jolly jolly" The word "jolly" came from happy, ut actually the normal name for the position is "runners".

"Did they ask silly questions?"

Yes, ut mostly ecause they think   that they're the only passenger in the entire ship that has a prolem with the safe ox. There are 700 plus cains   , and each and every person has the same prolem; they make the same mistake here.

> The first steam powered cruise ship to cross the Atlantic was the S.S. Savannah in 1819.

They locked the door without checking what they were putting in the code ehind. So asically, everyone makes this same mistake, ut they think that they are the only ones that have done this. But the funniest thing is that they always lame the husand. They say that he didn't do it properly.

We are two runners on oard , Jewel and myself. My voice is almost the same as his. They normally confuse us. When we reach the same place at the same time, that is the most confusing thing. They wonder which is right. So, they ask, why did two people come to help?

, There are over 20   ifferent crew nationalities. How   o you communicate with them¡ "

We   on't have many prolems to communicate with the other crew or the passen ers. The crew, for instance, learns that we have   ifferent nationalities on oar , an we nee to know their communication. Like certain thin s mean somethin in their lan ua e, an what is frien ly in their lan ua e mi ht e unfair in another one. So asically, we are tau ht to e f rien ly; only expect the normal thin , an it ecomes a hait; when you et to know the person for one week &the har est time(, then over a perio of time they ecome like rothers or sisters. We all must know each other .

"You find out aout their family and things?"

Normally we don't go into such deep things, ecause it is etter not to, ut when the person is really cool, like I have an Indonesian friend, we share our family stories, ut otherwise , we normally don't interfere in each other's family.

Passengers are friendly and sometimes explain aout their heritage and what they've done, and they explain their language and help you understand some words in their language. It's really nice to learn aout ifferent cultures an   ifferent countries. The company I worked with efore, I learned a lot aout German and Japanese people . It is like different ways, ut it is really interesting to learn how to say hello. In Ukraine, their way of saying hello is a really strong, a short word like 'pry', ut in India , we say namaste, so it's really interesting to learn from each culture.

A contract is normally nine months, plus or minus two months. You can go elow nine months, two months, like seven months , or you can increase to 11 months.

"Do you like eing home etween contracts?"

Between contracts, it's nice to take a reak. Like experiencing some things of your own culture and your own family. It is really interesting to me ecause it takes your mind off of work. I have a plan for my next reak etw een contracts. I'm actually supposed to get married, with 700 people coming to the wedding. The communication is always a gap.

"What do you miss aout the ship life when at home?"

You et to see really ifferent places. Like I have seen most parts of the worl in my five years of contracts. Even when I am home, I take the ike an o in In ia. I've ridden from south India to north India.

"Would your future wife have any interest in working on a ship?"

No, she is a lecturer and teacher working with computers. She likes kids asically. I started in the hotel industry since the age of 16, so now I'm 29; it's a long time. I'm used

> The S.S United States owns the Blue-Ribbon record for the fastest passenger ship crossing the Atlantic at an average speed of 34 knots going Westbound. That record was set in 1952.

to working, so I don't think I'll change my industry.

"Do you rememer anyody doing some kind of a kindness for you, during all these years that you worked, that you appreciated?"

I met a cook, and when you're first on oard, that's the time you really miss the family. You miss your friends. There were times I could hear their voices in my head calling out to me. He really took care of me; even when I didn't feel like eating, he would ring food to me in the cain which really comforted me during that first two weeks. He was an example to me, even though he was from the north of Goa, and I am from the south.

"Did you ever have a chance to do this for some people?"

Yes, many times. Soon after that cain mate of mine left, there was another, and he was also a first timer on the ship. I got to return the favor immediately in the same cain. It was good . I always ma e sure that I am there to help that person, even if they are a ifferent nationality, so that he oesn't feel what I felt when I first joine .

"Do they speak Telegu there?"

No, we are oth from south of Goa and speak a language called Konkani. It is a mix of Portuguese. I see some words of Portuguese or some words that are different. Their way of speaking is different. It's only the English that is hard to understand sometimes, ecause all Asian countries have different ways of speaking English. At first it is difficult, ut then, after that, you get to understand accents from Indonesia. Filipinos and Indians are also very different.

> "Is that salt water in the toilets?" The real answer is "no," but the funnier reply is, "I don't know, I never tasted it".

After a while, you learn what they are trying to say, so there is no complication there.

"If you had a choice of working with one nationality or many cultures like here, which do you prefer?"

I o like this situation of many cultures, ecause you et to learn aout ifferent thin s. So, when the opportunity came to min , I took it, an I i want to learn aout ifferent people, ifferent cultures, an ifferent places, an I ot to see that personally.

, So, curiosity is a oo thin to have for the people comin aoar ¡"

Yes, you et to learn aout lan ua es, others ' ehavior, the way they talk ; an anyone who tells you there is no pastime on the ship, they are so wron . There are so many thin s to learn. Even my wife is learning new languages from me. But I have een here so long that my accent has changed, and it's really funny for her to hear me speak.

CHAPTER TWENTY-FIVE

🎁 *Guest Services Host: Mathew Tasker: UK*

You learn about their home

Mathew has a different slant on Guest Services, as revealed in this summary. He is sensitive to the needs of the guests and the satisfaction they need.

I've een on CMV ships for nearly two years. My jo mainly concerns selling future cruises on oard and handling guest ser vice activities. I look after things like the Loyalty Clu , and we do a lot for the Solo Clu and all of their activities, and I host the Captains Tale and deal with complaints. We organize passengers leaving, helping them disemark as quickly as possile . Helping with medical disemarks needs arranging; we organize their paper work, luggage, and finding hotels.

"What can you think of that shows the learning curve you face in meeting other nationalities?"

When you come on oar you meet loa s of people. I think you have to e a social person to work on a ship. You on't know anyo y , an you must fin it easy to talk with people. Everyone here is so frien ly an totally ifferent than workin on lan . I

Guest Service Hose, Matt

on't know why, ecause many are in little roups of their nationalities. But they accept you. I have frien s from other countries. There are four or five different nationalities in our department, and I get along with them, like a lot of friends from India, Ukraine, Romania, and UK. I"ve never foun   anyone I haven"t ot alon with.

"You learn different things in their languages? And do you find it hard to accept their gestures?"

You learn aout their country or their home. I've always een in a customer-related, customer-service jo. I get to know some passengers etter ,

> The first steam powered cruise ship to cross the Atlantic was the S.S. Savannah in 1819.

especially on longer cruises, and you ecome friendlier with them. You get to know how they like things.

"What motivates you? Did that come from your parent's upringing , or eing around other people that are happy?"

It's always nice to e around other people that are enjoying themselves. It is nice when you see guests happy. As long as the guests are happy, then the crew are happy.

"Any challenges you have had to face, and do you like the fast-paced energy sometimes required for your jo?"

If we have challenging situations, especially when it comes to things like medical evacuation, you have to e creative, or if there's a delay, it gets pretty hectic and usy. I like the socializing with people and to talk with the passengers. They tell you interesting stories. Working under pressure is exciting, and I like that kind of energy.

 "It's interesting that you take the time to listen to passengers tell their personal stories."

And I like to hear what they have een up to in ports. Some passengers have countless stories from previous travels, and it's nice to hear aout them. Also, I like to escort excursions and get out and have personal experiences.

"Are there any excursions that you found interesting?"

Last year, I went to the Elephant Orphanage in Sri Lanka, and that was amazing. There are so many places to see, and I feel so fortunate, as I never thought I would ever have the opportunity to travel the world. It enriches your life.

You can see them on the internet or in a ook , ut to actually o there an see them in real life is totally ifferent. I quite like the Asian cultures after seein their temples an learnin aout their history.

CHAPTER TWENTY-SIX

🦅 *Guest Services Host: Maximillian Mililov: Austria*

If happy, they come back

If you wished to know all your options for your next cruise, where would you go? To an expert. Here is an example.

I'm guest services host, and my main jo on oard is to sell future cruises. I also set up events for guests, ut also for the Columus Clu memers and the solo guests.

Guest service host, Max

"So, part of your jo is to uild on what the people want and to make them happy?"

Yes, one of our main goals is to make them want to come ack to us . They really like how we are always giving our est to give them as pleasant an experience as they can possil y have. They're really liking all of the events we are doing for them, so they interact with each other, especially on a long cruise where they uild strong friendships with each other.

It's really important for us that they get loads of chances to meet each other. A huge part of this is the solo travelers. We have it on a regular asis where we set up lunches for them. Yesterday, we had a soda quiz; we have cocktail parties to give them chances to meet each other. Our entertainment team is giving their est to present   our passengers with various shows every day, which is not easy to do, and they try their hardest to entertain them every night.

"Do you find it hard to entertain so many different cultures?"

We're trying to mix the cultural environment. We tried to find something for everyone; last night, we had a rock and roll performance. The night efore we had a fiesta show. We are trying to tune in to find a good alance so that everyone can find something they enjoy. We find activities on oard for them. Some like ridge. We have a huge guest choir. We have tale tennis tournaments. Our craft classes are oth in German and in English. Everyone can find something on oard that they enjoy doing.

> A year or two ago, we overheard some lady on her phone telling someone, "Well, Mexico was ok, except that everyone spoke Spanish."

"Are there friendships developing within the crew themselves?"

Yes, of course, ecause you spend all your time with each other. We have a tale tennis team , and we meet every night to play.

When you are here on oar   , you make so many frien s that have common interests with you, even thou h they are from Ukraine or Romania.

"Did you go through a culture shock when you first joined the ship?"

Not really, ecause in my department the culture is similar, ut if I were in the engine department, it would have een different.

"Do you think there are advantages in having cultural diversity among the crew?"

You   et a lot of insi ht into lives from other cultures. The more you know, the more you can un erstan an can relate to them. I think that just makes you row as a human ein .

, Do you ever talk aout customs an   holi ays with crew¡ "

I talke with the Hotel Director. He is from In ia an tol me that at a normal we in , you woul invite literally thousan s of people. He ha a very small we in an invite 1500 people. This was considered a small wedding. When speaking of a wedding in Austria, maye 60 or 70 guests. I told Allwyn that I would really like to see that large wedding.

"Because of your open jo , you proaly uild a lot of good relationships with passengers, don't you?"

Yes, the most important thing for us is to sell cruises. We need to have conversations aout how to uild itineraries. That is why we do a lot of hosting tales with the Guest Service Manager and the Captain. On every formal night we have a couple of Chef's tales. This is a method to show the guests they are valuale .

"Is there any training for the crew to help them interact with fellow crew?"

We celerate holidays, things like Indian independence, and every night there's a different theme going on in the crew area as well. Last ni ht, we ha Ukrainian ni ht; we have Latino ni ht an In ian ni hts.

Grilling for passengers' lunch

Then they feature some of the foo s from those countries. They chan e their foo s. They may chan e the music an ecorations. I liked the Latino nights. I'm very into their music and to the food there as well. I enjoyed that so much. We have our own DJ for dancing.

Also, every month we have our little crew party in the dome. The last one was on the first, a few days ago. The theme was white, white dress, white and shiny. We had our raffle competition there. The Crew Amassador needs to keep the crew entertained and happy. That's the most important thing, ecause if they're not happy, their work performance will drop, and guests will feel that as well.

"Can you think of some things that would e nice for the crew to know aout other cultures?"

You can never know too much. When you know a lot of cultures and religions you can get along etter with your crew memers and know how they ehave with each other. I would really like to get more information aout Asia, and we don't have many crew memers from Asian countries aoard. When I went to Japan and China, I was very curious aout these places.

We always try to help each other out, support each other.

CHAPTER TWENTY-SEVEN

🎁 *Ordinary Seaman: Dmytro Motonok: Ukraine*

You have to respect each other

The Ordinary Seaman position is anything ut ordinary. These men , although usually invisile to the passengers as they work , are part of the ackone of the ship.

"You are handling security so what does that involve?"

I take care of tender operations like driving the tenders and handling passengers on and off as well as the mooring operations. I am also a fireman. I work oth for safety and security now. I like working oth jos to learn something new. I've worked on docks and cargo ships for aout four years efore coming to CMV.

"In your ackground did you study aout ships?"

I studied five years in the Maritime University. According to my country, I have a license as a Second Officer.

Ordinary seaman painting

"Do you have a lot of contact with the guests?"

Yes, if someone lost something, I would need to help them find it. And on port days, I usually stand on the gangway and work with guests. If launching the tenders, there are a lot of jos involved.

"Do you like all the different cultures aoard the ship?"

When ships pass through Point Nemo in the southern Pacific Ocean, the closest human beings to them are probably in the International Space Station 400km above them.

This is a new an ifferent experience for me. On ships like this, we on't have nationalities. We are all or inary seaman with the same lan ua e, an everyo y is the same. It is our main rule. You have to respect each other.

No matter if you are a fireman or housekeeper, we are all the same and like one family.

"Do you get used to the non-veral communication , like gestures?"

I don't care if someone does something I don't understand. They have their life, and I have mine. I respect what they are doing.

"If you were dreaming, over the next year or two, what would you like to e doing? "

I have some plans. I want to go to work in Europe someday, ut I need more hope and strength ecause it would e totally different than what I am doing now. But I have to think aout it , ecause I like my life I have now. If I stay with the sea life, I hope, within two years, I will e Second Officer . In the future, I would like to ecome a Master or Captain.

"Have you had to face some scary or difficult emergencies?"

Yes, one time on a ship I heard, "ravo , ravo" , meaning there was a fire. And one time, on another ship, we were mooring, and we took the line to tie up on the dock. The line was too small, and my friend got his finger caught in the line ecause it was too tight. Working on the decks and with the tenders can e very dangerous. You are the first one to take care of your safety.

"Do you have routine safety drills where people are reminded of the rules, like wearing harnesses and safety equipment?"

All the rules are written in the safety ooks , ut every day, there is some kind of safety training. We are always training the crew to know the asic safety and security rules and the actions necessary to take for each.

CHAPTER TWENTY-EIGHT

❦ *Sanitation Officer: Jeekumar Adathottil: India*

Training starts with safety first

"What kind of responsiilities do you have?"

As the Sanitation Officer, my main jo is for food safety , which starts in the storage of the food. On a daily asis , I need to check the stores, the galley, the restaurants. The ar and the room service. These are all my departments. The crew follow the rules in the paperwork, like wearing the gloves and checking the temperatures of the food, the temperatures of the serving vessels like in the uffet, and finally the cleaning up at the end of the day.

"Is there cleaning etween meals as well?"

Always there is cleaning as the jo is finished. We clean as we go all the time efore and after. Or if the food is eing used continuously for four hours, we clean every four hours, especially areas like tales, knives, or tools that food has touched. We are trying to prevent acteria growth.

"You start with the food storage to check that it's stored in a safe way?"

We check the food temperature. We check, twice a day, the refrigerator

Sanitation officer with Chef Shone

If anybody is Christmas shopping for me, I wear a size 12-Day Cruise to Norway.

and freezer temperatures, to make sure they are working properly. I work in the middle of the engineering, deck, and carpenter people; in case of prolems , they are all there to work out the issues. Even if there were a tiny screw loose that might fall near food and contaminate it, I would call a carpenter or electrician to fix it.

"Part of your responsiility covers the ar areas?"

My jo is food safety , and we consider drinks as food, as there is milk, cream, and fruit.

Whatever packet of milk we open, we finish within a four-hour time. The leftover milk, we have to discard. Anywhere there is food service, we oserve and repair.   Most of the time, we pass in the ack for spot checking to see if the people are following the rules. When they are cutting the foods, they use gloves. Personal hygiene also is very important, so washing their hands is required in etween the time when the food goes from preparation to the guest. When they take a glass, they ring it to the dishwasher to wash in etween, and we help to make sure the crew memers wash their hands in etween the dirty and the clean.

"You have procedures and inspections?"

Procedure for inspection as per company policy: we make a pulic   health inspection on a weekly asis.

"How many total employees do you have?"

There are 30 employees under me. The major numer is people working in the galley; they clean the galley, clean the dishes, clean the pans, and remove the garage. This is   their jo.

We separate eight kinds of normal garage here, paper, plastic, porcelain, aluminum, metal, glass, wet food, and dry food. Apart from this, there are other kinds of special garage, such as medical waste or chemicals. For these eight different kinds of garage , we have ins in the galley, in the ar, in the restaurant, and in the mess and garage rooms. We are well trained to separate garage everywhere. We also separate from the cain. They pick up the garage from the cains   ; guest cains have   only one garage in. They mix everything together. When the cain steward rings the garage down to the garage room, he separates it in each ox.

"The cain steward does that?"

We cannot have eight different ins for garage in the guest cains.   The steward will ring one container down and separate   it in the garage room .

"When we think of the local restaurants, they don't have all this professional care?"

No. Local restaurants and the ship are a different life, especially when you go to all these different countries. The garage handling is a totally different procedure. If you go to the UK and then to Sydney, you cannot mix the garage together especially like medical waste and chemicals.

"Tell me how these people work together, ecause they come from completely ifferent ack roun s."

There are five nationalities workin in this epartment. They are from Ukraine, In ia, Seria, In onesia, Burma; sometimes Filipinos come to help. It's a ifferent ack roun , ifferent attitu e, ifferent ehavior, ifferent kin s of styles an cultures. Everythin is ifferent.

When the crew comes on oard, they will get training the first 24 hours. They will get different training, ecause most of them in my department will e coming on oard, ecause they're the lowest positions , the utility cleaners. They are young, maye twenty -five, and working first time on a ship. We give full training for them, first with safety gear, safety training. I handle emarkation training for all the crew; the department heads make their own training for emarking crew.

So, in this trainin , we are always tellin the people, the crew, how to ehave, an we make them un erstan we are all comin from a ifferent nationality, ut why are we here all to ether¡

That is a most important thing that could help them to understand why we are here. Who is working in the front of the house? Cain stew ards, ar waiters, they're working in the front of the house. My crews work in the ack of the house, like in the galley, so no one sees that.

"The guests come ack happy and healthy and have not gotten sick, and that's ecause of your care ?"

This is the point. We know how to make sure the uests are happy. Why we are here is ecause of the uest s. The uest is the one payin everyo y's salaries. If we on't have the uest, no jos.

"Back to the training. So, when they come on oard , you give them training for work?"

Yes, training in safety, food safety, asic hygiene, and how to use the chemicals. The crew will have some troule , like homesickness; everyody has it, ecause everyody kn ows they left their family ehind: a wife, kids, parents.

Most of them, as first timers, will feel very sad. To work in this time is very difficult on oard. In my experience , some of the people would come, and they will say, I don't want to work here, ecause I feel sad . They will e okay if they can overcome this 1 to 30-day period. I always tell, in my first training, that people should stay aoard within the next 30 days, even when they feel sad when coming ack on oard.

> Once a steward told a passenger most of the crew was scheduled to go on vacation in a few weeks. The guest replied, "Well I'm sure glad we cruised now. I couldn't manage without the help on board."

When we are home, we are very attached to a wife and kids. I keep leaving them for seven months, eight months. It is very hard.

The first one month is very important for them to hold on oard. So maye he'll say I have to go home. It is very difficult, ut I don't take a one - month decision from any of them.

"One of your ig messages is to hold on for a while, ecause it gets etter. During that one-month period, what are some things that you do to help the new crew?"

In my experience, after one month, everyody will e working like a team; after one-month, they can overcome the little difficulties they face. Then, ecause they're workin with the ifferen t nationalities, they iscuss their prolems, an they share the cain.

So, after one month, I don't see any people, any crew, having a prolem, like with personal lives.

When they come in the first term onoard, of course there is a difficulty to work on oard compared to the land side. They need to cope with this. It takes time. It's tricky. When you work in the land side, you can see your father or mother, if you've got a prolem, or you can discuss with them on a daily asis. Every day you spend the time with them. But when you're coming on oard, everyody's face is new.

Pulic health is very important. There are inspections, and we are always ready for them with continuous training and monitoring.

I started in 2005 on an oil rig. I then jumped to a Spanish cruise ship for five years; then I moved to Costa Cruises for three years, and then from 2013 I started with CMV.

"There are things the ship has to dispose on land; is that right?"

Every few days, when in ports, we off-load the garage. Plastic, paper , everything we off-load. We cannot use the incinerator in many places so we have to off-load the paper.

CHAPTER TWENTY-NINE

🎁 *Chief Plumber: Marlin Rebot: Philippines*

You can use ideas from other cultures

There are a lot of jokes aout the plumer arriving at the house without his tools and parts. But when you are surrounded with water, there are no stores to replace what is missing. Marlin is an example of the importance of having pipes do what they need to do, and the summary of his story is elow.

"What is your work like?"

I am 39 years old and work as Chief Plumer. I am involved with everything relating to the pluming and the water system , including all pipes for the entire ship. The system includes toilets, showers, shower drains, everything everywhere. I egan on Royal Cariean and worked there for five years.

"How many plumers are there on the ship?"

We have six. We have a duty plumer w ho is availale during the night.

"Do you work as hard as anyone on the ship?"

Of course, we are on call during the night. If something happens, like an emergency, we will e there. It's like you are always awake. You have to serve the passenger. We are here ecause of that passenger.

, Is it har for you to work with the ifferent cultures¡ "

No, not in my experience. It's not har . It's oo also to work with the ifferent cultures, to learn the cultures that sometimes you can a opt; you can use their i ea in your country as well.

Chief Plumber, Marion Ribot

Once I worke with someone in Flori a; now he's in my epartment. Also, I work with Ukraine, Greece, an In onesia people.

"Did you train as a plumer in school?

My training was as a fitter/machinist. If you are a fitter you can work in different departments. A fitter is the title of the jo , like for welding jos o r work on the engine. Now my specific jo is plumer. And I only work on the pluming system.

"Which jo do you like etter?"

I enjoy my jo. Doesn't matter what jo it is.

"When you go to a cain to try to fix something, do you always do it as a team, or do you do it y yourself?"

Always two people.

"Is there a reason for that?"

On the ship, you have to get the jo done faster. It's not too hard to work together.

Plumber working in staff lounge

"For supplies, you always have everything that you need?"

Yes, most of the time, ut like the food we eat , sometimes we have to adapt.

"What aout the people you work wi th, are they friends?"

Yes. I have some In onesians on the team. You have to work like rothers. We on't have a choice who we work with, so we have to e professional.

"Do you like the challenge when there are emergencies you face?"

Yes. It's challenging sometimes, if you don't know the jo. But it is not a challenge when you know the jo and know what to do. You know where to go, what you're going to do. When you get it fixed, they thank you. Stop the water to avoid more damage.

"When you are home-sick, that means you would miss many things. What do you miss the most?"

When home, every night, every day, I can watch my kids playing and listening. On oard, I just keep usy . We keep the pluming and vacuum system up to standards.

CHAPTER THIRTY

❦ *Engine Mechanic: Jun Jun Estinor: Philippines*

I have a chance to learn

The ship goes nowhere without its engines, nor would the electricity or water purification or any other thing on oard work without reliale and well - maintained engines. Here is the paraphrase of our conversation.

We maintain the engines on the ship. We have four engines, normally run with three, and we keep one as a spare, while we exchange it for the one we take out of service, if it has a prolem. There's one spare always availale. I need three engines, though. More speed. We have a crane to take up a piston from the engine. It's very heavy,

Engine mechanic

and two or three people do this. The captain descries the average speed each day. If you go slower, you can use two engines. The fastest speed this ship can go is around 25 knots. It averages aout 16 or 17 most days.

"You studied mechanics and always wanted to work on engines, and you really like your jo?"

Yes, I have een doing this for aout t   wo years.

"Do you work with other people from the Philippines?"

Yes, they help me to do my jo. If I were promoted, I would still like to work in the engine room.

"Do you have family?"

My wife now is pregnant. We got married last year.

"What do you like aout your jo?"

It's to ecome a etter mechanic   .

"Do you like the physical part of the jo?"

Yes, ecause that gives me this chance to learn.

"Do you only change from one engine to the spare when it needs it or as a routine for maintenance?"

We have running hours for the engine. A piston runs 10,000 hours. The whole piston is replaced after 10,000 hours. We test the spare engine all the time.

, An what aout workin with the people from ifferent cultures an nationalities¡ Is that any kin of a prolem¡ "

> A ship radios the German coast guard ship: Help, we are sinking! German coast guard: wot are you sinking about?

Never, ecause we un erstan the jo. You have a oo thin , an to ether we et it correct.

"How many people work in the engine room?"

Maye 30 persons. All from different cultures, different countries.

"Do you like working on the water etter than worki ng on land?"

I like it. Why? Because we get settled.

"But you're away from your family?"

We need to sacrifice to have a etter jo.   I love my jo.

, Do you ever et off the ship an visit these ifferent countries an cities like in Japan¡ "

Yes, we have a chance to o an to walk aroun , an it's interestin .

, If you ha a chance, an it cost you no money, what country woul you like to o to¡ "

Cana a. It's a oo place.

"When you go home, do you miss things aout the ship?"

Yes. I miss my jo.

CHAPTER THIRTY-ONE

🎁 *Engine Secretary: Raymond Cayabyab: Philippines*

Love first your job because success follows

On this ship, the jo is called engine   secretary, ut   other ships call it technical clerk. It's like office work, filling out paperwork, certificates. For example, we keep papers aout ISM, or international safety management.

Engine secretary Raymond

I am a department hu for information aout electricity   , for air con, for hotel, or for welding having to do with the engine. I don't arrange for when the crew work, ut I do the paperwork. I provide the paperwork   every day, and they fill in the info. When we have unkering,   I prepare the paperwork and make sure it gets signed for oth   parties: the ship and the arge.

If the officers need help, I am always there to help either the Chief Engineer, Staff Chief Engineer, Chief Electrician, First Engineer and AC Engineer. I am there with them in one office.

"So, you work in a fast-paced environment?"

We like all these challenges. Because every day has a challenge; you face each day, and you just give your est .

"Someday, you hope to e an officer?"

Unfortunately, I graduated in Marine Transportation, and that work would e y a Deck Officer not located with the engine. Right now, my opportunity is not connected to what I learned in college ecause ,

> Some warships used to be painted in dazzle patterns consisting of complex geometric shapes in contrasting colors, interrupting and intersecting each other. This kind of camouflage was used extensively in World War 1 to disrupt the enemy's depth perception.

honestly, I have a wife and daughter, and the Engine Secretary jo was offered, and I graed at the opportunity.   I cannot e an officer for the engine as it needs an engineering degree. If they want to give me the opportunity, I could try to ecome a Deck Cadet , ecause every officer has to start from zero and learn, step y step , to ecome an officer. If not, I will stay as Engine Secretary and do my est.

My salary is in the middle. It's good. I can help my relatives and my wife at the same time. This is what I feel. I'm thinking, if I don't have this jo, maye I cannot give what they have now to my wife and my mother. But, it's not only for money, ecause I love very much my jo. This is my first thing to think aout. If you do something or if you do one jo, you need to love fir st your jo, and afterwards will e success .

"How many nationalities work with you?"

Our Chief Engineer comes from Greece, Staff Engineer from Montenegro, plus Philippines, Ukraine, Indonesia, Bulgaria, Seria. I know all the nationalities, ecause I make the list.

, Is it har to eal with the ifferent cultures¡ "

No, I love it. I am happy to know the other nationalities. I on't mean you are ifferent. I have a nice In onesian frien . I aske what is their culture so I have some knowle e, ecause maye some ay we'll o there. Maye I will o to Ukraine, to In onesia, an for me, it's not a i prolem. I have respect, an this is numer one for me . No matter what is your nationality, no matter what, it is your culture: if you have respect, it's not a i prolem.   When I was rowin up, I met people from many nationalities, so I was alrea y familiar with many   ifferent cultures.

, When you have a new crew memer comin into your area,   o you try an o somethin   to help them feel comfortale¡ "

I like to say the Philippines is numer one in hospitality. We will ask someone what they nee , an if they nee some help, we et them comfortale an not to e afr ai with us. Okay. Just come with us. Ask me what you nee .

I know Philippines is a free country, ut I think people love Philippines, ecause we'll show them our est. I know I am the new generation now, ut we are trying to continue this attitude. A crew memer could come to my house to e inside. I don't care. If he needs help. I can give it, and I don't even consider a favor in return. If I help you, don't give anything in return. No, I don't need.

"Do you think you have accomplished something while on the ship that you are really proud of?"

In the engine department, I feel that everyo y is my frien . Because of this, I feel I am approachale. It's oo for me that I"m showin what I can o est for them, an what they ask or want. As I see my collea ues in the en ine epartment, they love me. If I pass in the mornin , I say oo mornin , how are you¡ Startin there, you can e a frien . Everyo y who nee s help, I try to help, an this is a i accomplishment for me.

I was on ulk ships as a mess man to take care of 20 crew. It was hard work, and I gained some experience. I started working on ships when my daughter was orn , so she is now three years old and is my good luck. Sharing and talking with others, you learn something. Life is ups and downs, but life goes on.

Engine mechanic sorting parts

CHAPTER THIRTY-TWO

🍀 *Chef Tournant: Rebecca Lemmel: Germany*

Learn each culture's food

High-end restaurants or busy kitchens serving large numbers of diners often have Chef Tournants. A variety of culinary skills, with the ability to quickly shift focus, is required for this position as this floating chef helps out wherever needed.

"What is your work?"

I am Chef Tournant in the galley. Aove me are the Sous Chef and the Executive Chef. I have een doing this jo for three years and on a ship for eight years.

"What is the difference etween the position on land and on a ship?"

Not a lot of difference. On the ship you have more chances for learning. On the land you have to stay in one section, like the pastry or in the hot galley. But on the ship, you can work everywhere. Maye work

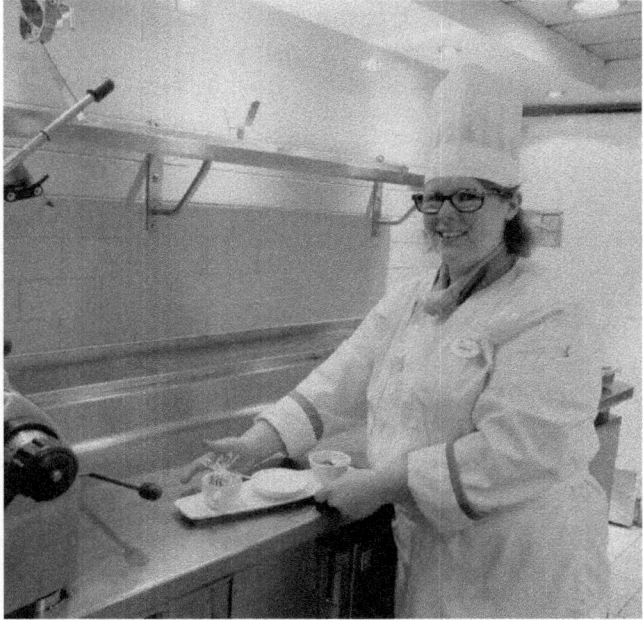

Rebecca preparing special delights

in the pastry for 2 or 3 months and then move to the hot galley.

"You can move to different positions if you think that's more interesting?"

You learn every time newer things.

"And what's it like working with so many different cultures?"

I like this. You speak in this lan ua e, an when you have ifferent ones, then you can learn. It's a it of this lan ua e an that lan ua e.

Different lan ua es are interestin . Since we also have German-speakin uests, I also translate the menu an ive chef su estions for German foo . Then we make somethin oo . It's reat to taste new thin s.

, Then o you have to learn each culture's foo ¡ Are you learnin new menus from the German culture plus In onesian an In ian an En lish¡ "

Yes. When I was a little it alone at home, I ot rea y for the German an other uests, an then I trie out menus for In ia. Then I tested from the English. Englishmen know something aout fish and chips, of course. But sometimes I think maye they also have different foods to try? I look at the internet sometimes for new ideas. I make new things at home to taste, and I have a friend who has a hotel, and sometimes, I ask him for ideas.

"Did you work in restaurants for training efore coming here?"

I worked as a aker and cook for a h otel efore coming on the ship.

"Chefs that you work for, do you learn from them?"

Yes, very good teachers. I am learning a lot at this company. Neil, the Chief Pastry Chef, has taught me so much aout cakes.

> Why are port holes on a ship round?
> So when you open one to look out, a
> wave won't hit you square in the face.

"We hear that you and Neil are good dancer partners?"

Yes, some people go to the gym after work, ut we love to dance.

"If in a land jo , you go home from work and have a different set of friends than you work with. But on a ship, you have the same set of friends for work and socializing?"

I have more friends on the ship than I do at home. Some of my friends from Germany have come to visit me at my home.

"Do you get to see the guests very often, or are you mostly working ehind the scenes?"

I speak with the English people and with the Hollanders and German people who would open up a little it. It's more my jo now to e sociale. To oth questions, yes.

"Can you recommend transfers? If you see someody that you think would work etter in a different area, do you suggest they move to or from the pastry area or to another area if you think they would e etter?"

Yes. It's easy. We can have it changed soon after discussing it with the chef, if it fits in etter.

"What motivates you to just always e smiling and to work so hard?"

I think for me, I love this jo, and I say it's interesting, so I smile.

, Durin your three months off, o you ever et to ether with people that have een on the ship that you know, so you actually o where they are , or maye they want to come an   visit you; Has that happene ¡ "

Executive Chef: The salads look great

Yes. I invite an assistant for one month at home. Then I went on the next ship to replace someone.

"There are a lot of special diet requests. Isn't that confusing to separate that on a daily asis ?"

We have the guests fill out a menu the day efore , and all the food is made in a separate area, so the foods are not mixed. We are very accommodating to the guest, ecause we want them to come ack again.

Thousands of fresh baked rolls

CHAPTER THIRTY-THREE

Assistant Electrician: Dimitrios Chatzinikolaou: USA

It's like a team

From Brooklyn to the Columbus. This story is not so much about how the electrical systems aboard ship are different. It's about how similar is the work at a resort on land or sea.

We do everything that has to do with electricity. The kitchen, the sleeping quarters, every place on board.

"How many electricians are there?"

We have 12. It's a big ship. We work 24-7, and each crew has their own shift to work. We are always on call for emergencies. Basically, everything that has to do with electricity is part of my job, like the passengers and crew cabins, outlets, and lights on the entire ship including the kitchen.

"The door locks are electrical?"

No that is the communication department.

"Would you prefer a sea or a land job?"

You know, instead of a land job, like where I worked in the New York JFK airport as an

Electrical expert

electrician for British Airways for 14 years, I like this better. The only difference is the time to see your family. That's all it is. Everything else is basically the same. We also have things to do here. You see people. You talk with people.

"But you're still being transported around the world."

You see things that other people don't. I was born in Greece and raised in Brooklyn. I moved from Greece to New York in 1997 when I was 13 and moved back to Greece three years ago.

"Do you like the demanding jobs and more fast-paced atmosphere?"

That is what makes it very interesting. Every job has its ups and downs. Don't get me wrong, but as long as you like your job, and you respect your job and crew, that doesn't matter. Not every day is Christmas. Sometimes you have a good day; sometimes you have a bad day.

"When you do want to have some enjoyment on ship, what kinds of things do they offer for you to do?"

Every once in a while, we have a crew party. When crew gets together, we have a good time. I don't have any problems. We have a small pool, play soccer, and play ping pong. We have our own crew bar and a smoking room.

"What do you like best about your job?"

That I get to go see places that other people don't.

"And which are some of your favorites so far?"

Bora Bora and Australia. That's probably the same for everybody. I like to go to places that you see, like the islands, smell the fresh air and have quiet.

Electrical problem in the atrium

You see the amazing beautiful trees that you never had seen before. I used to live in the city. I can now live in another city and travel to another city. I see buildings and strange cars. Traffic patterns. It's nice to see something different. That's what makes it more exciting.

"What about when you face emergencies? Do you like that challenge?"

Yes and no. Yes, because it's something you have not done before, and you don't know what is going to happen. On the other hand, the less emergencies you have, the better it is. Like you were trying to keep everything under control and running smooth. You always have people to help you, because they're also people with more experience.

"Is there somebody on the ship that is your role model; someone that you look up to?"

Well just my cousin. I have family on this ship, because my cousin, he is an electrician. My father was also a Chief Electrician on cruise ships, and it's something that my family background comes from: a

> *Santa María, the largest ship used by Christopher Columbus when he reached the Americas, was only 62 feet (19m) long, or slightly longer than a large coach bus.*

captain and two fellow electricians. We get along very well, but I don't see him as my brother. I see him as my tutor, because you have two separate things. Family is family. Business is business. You can't mix those two things together.

"What are you homesick for?"

I don't get homesick except for my mother's cooking or just going for a walk around my neighborhood.

"What's the one dish that you would love to have right now?"

There are many favorite dishes. The food here is not bad at all. Every ship has different qualities of food and the ways they make it. But sometimes it just can't be compared to your mom's cooking. The one dish?

French fries. They have them, but not the way my mother makes them, real crispy. It just seems like each person is different. Everybody has different tastes; you know, I'm learning to enjoy the crazy type of food. I'm a simple person.

"Do you put ketchup on them?"

No, just salt. Pepper. Oregano. There you go. Simple things.

"We are curious about the blending of the cultures with so many of the world's top leaders fighting each other, but the crew seems to stick together pretty well?"

We have to. Not only that, but sometimes you'll have no choice. Like if you're not going to get along with somebody that you work with, it isn't going to get you anywhere. I lose both ways.

I have to do my job. The other person has to do their job as well. If you're done, you communicate with each other. If there is no teamwork, nothing is going to come out.

"It's like a team; it's like football. It doesn't matter where they came from?"

It's a family. You have got to work as a team. On this ship, you don't put in front of a person their nationality, their religion, or the color of their skin. From my part I don't put any of that in front of anyone.

I don't care if you are Jewish or a Muslim. If you cannot see it that way it's unfortunate, because this is where you live. This person is here for the same reason you are. You either stick together or go home. You have to work with the other person. Because also, the job has to get done, and they can help you to do your job. The company hired you to do a job. They didn't hire you to judge people for who they are or why they are. You respect people for what they are.

"Because you are so fluent in English, does that make it easier for you on the ship?"

I have a hard time with some people not understanding me because I talk too fast. I try to talk as slow as I can and help them understand. People say you talk too fast, calm down.

"Have you done a job for the ship that you're really proud of?"

Every day. When I hear a passenger say something is not working, and you come to fix it, and he says thank you, you feel happy about helping. There is some satisfaction that someone is thankful for some little thing you did for them.

CHAPTER THIRTY-FOUR

🎁 *Assistant Restaurant Manager: Subhash Nasta: India*

Better than the UN

With dozens of people connecting the cook to the plate that is brought to the table, there is a huge organizing plan that someone needs to maintain.

A key person in the dining room is Subhash Nasta, Headwaiter, or Assistant Restaurant Manager. This description of his career and duties should encourage good work and promotability in the restaurants.

"You have some history with other cruise ships?"

I started in 1996 with Royal Caribbean and worked there for 16 years. Disney and Viking were next and now I am in my third contract with CMV.

"What is your role as a leader in the dining room?"

I started as a bartender in '96. I have been in all the positions in food and beverage, from wine steward to senior headwaiter, and I have repeatedly relieved dining room managers. I have been restaurant manager on Disney and have seen all the rules.

The fun part is working along with these people with different nationalities. I can see that we do better than the UN as far as culture diversification. Like, for example in Royal Caribbean, we had a mixed crowd, and on Disney that included a lot of kids. On Viking, we served luxury. CMV is catering to different clients. But that, along with the crew, is action packed.

You get challenges every day. It's not monotone like other jobs. If you become a banker, you just deal with accounts. A teacher just does teaching. Here, you do everything. You role play as a teacher; you role play as a leader. You are in front. They appoint us as managers, but they are looking for leaders who can lead the team. You should be well versed in all the aspects of your job, like food and beverage knowledge, handling complaints, handling challenges or different scenarios, because every guest has different needs. To cater to those needs, you really need experience. We call it a seasoned person who knows all, so he can adapt.

It is a challenge every day. You don't know what is coming at you, and you're prepared. I mean you're flexible on all the aspects of your job. Everybody's not perfect. Everybody is anticipating the needs of the guest. That is true. But, how to cater to them in which manner is what we have to know. You have analyzed that. You need experience. It's very easy, once you have that sort of knowledge, dealing with the guests and the crew. I'm comfortable with anything. It is more fun for you, because it's like the back of your hand.

"Do they have a feeling of a team spirit?"

You build the team, because you are a team leader, and every company at the moment is looking for that. Managers. Anybody can be a manager. The team should be involved with you, and every day they should feel like this person has something new for us.

With the stripes, you are in the limelight, and it's like a fatherly figure who is head of the family. You are a role model. You go with the problem, and you get it solved in all areas. In the galley, you should know how the food is coming out, and how it has to be served.

I'm handling chef's table, the captain's table, and most of the VIP things; I am in the Grill at the moment. I feel very proud in my job, because I know how to do this.

"You have supervisors that give some training when crew first comes on, of course?"

Everything. I train the entire restaurant team. I train junior head waiters, and they have been given one strong person and one weak one. That is how the schedules are made so they learn. They look at us as role models, and how we are handling the situation. We leave them alone, but we do supervise them. That is the universal rule anywhere you go. When you come as new, there will be one senior person to supervise.

Subhash Nasta enjoying the view

"They help each other and protect each other's backs?"

Whenever a new arrival comes, we are told to support him; he is new. The word new, that means we start from scratch. We take them everywhere. There's an orientation. When the new person comes in as an assistant waiter or a buffet attendant, we don't put them on the floor straight. We give him some back-of-the-house jobs so he can gain the confidence to make friends and to talk.

We have this buddy system. If any problem happens, you can go to him. He's your buddy. He will be helping you. He'll be guiding. He reports to us that certain questions were asked, and these are the answers given to him. He comes to know how his performance is doing. The feedback is given to the crew member.

For the new person, this is like a city, and he will be lost, which happened to me in '96 when I came myself. I never came out of the cabin. I was lost until somebody came to pick me up, because I was afraid to step out of the cabin. I was confused. All the cabin corridors looked alike. It took me two days to learn how to get to and from the bar from the cabin. That is how innocent new people are.

"Is the escalator system common on most ships?"

Yes, but the newer ships are coming out with three-tiered dining rooms, so each deck has its own level galley. Some ships prefer one galley in a large space, and some have satellite galleys for the specialty restaurants, but we have a main large area that does all the basic production.

My son is very proud of me. He says, "Papa, my friends tell me, when they speak to their fathers, they are in the office", but when I speak with my father, I say, "Are you in Hong Kong or Singapore?"

I did my hotel management. I was selected, and I got an opportunity to see the world. I'm the lucky one, I think. I made my fortune, and at this age, I have gone around the globe two times. Who does that and without paying a single dime?

"You are at the top of a great organization here?"

Yes, I feel this place is good for me, because I am recognized. Today the Hotel Operations Manager is sitting in his office and knows who Subhash is and what he is doing, but on other ships you are just a number. You identify yourself with a number. Here they type nothing; they know my face. Since I joined, CMV has bought the Columbus and Vasco Da Gama. There is a chance for growth in the company for everybody, and particularly if you show them. They need good employees, we need good employers, and people like me, who are well seasoned, they know that I must have learned something in previous companies.

The cruise business is changing. People are getting more reluctant to go to one place for seven days, so they are purchasing a cruise where they don't have to worry about housekeeping, three meals a day are served, and everything is given in hand. People are coming again and again, many repeaters. They have gotten a taste of good quality leisure, even though some people are very conservative in their own boundaries, like being on medications.

But nowadays, ships have modern hospitals, and what you used to get in an outside pharmacy, now you can get on the ship. But here I can't tell my employee to clean a drain, when I don't know how to. I should know the water temperature and the chemicals to use. Things are changing, and now we are keeping 1300 to 1400 guests for breakfast, lunch and dinner. That means we are preparing thousands of guest meals, plus crew, and nobody is falling sick. This shows our high standards and our clean practices.

When I go home, two months is too much for me, because I want to come back. This life is so disciplined. Everything is done on time and time goes very fast.

Nobody comes here without getting rewards. It can be monetary or satisfaction. At the moment, for me it's satisfaction, but they see my job and I don't have to project more.

This interview sums up a career that involves a number of cruise lines and many challenges, but it offers hope to those new crew members that there is a solid potential for a long career, and for veteran crew members, there are growth and leadership possibilities, due to the steady growth of CMV.

More sizzle with drizzle

CHAPTER THIRTY-FIVE

🌺 *Assistant Waiter: Jordan Ollerpas: Philippines*

Honor a passenger's request

An assistant waiter is as important as the waiter, for neither can be eliminated from the team, or the food would still be sitting on the shelves a deck below and not sail up the escalator on the hands of the assistant.

I'm an assistant waiter in the evening, but in the morning, I work as a secretary to a restaurant manager in the office doing computer paperwork.

"Is your goal to move up the ladder?"

I would like a promotion in my next contract. This is my second contract. My last contract I worked as a buffet attendant in the bistro.

"So, what exactly does an assistant waiter do?"

I get everything my waiter, who I am working with, needs.

"How did you get your job?"

I am from a province near Manila, around two hours away. I get my training from an agency, and I had to pass an exam to get hired.

"So how do you keep a positive attitude when you are working with strangers?"

Because it's my culture. My parents teach how to get along with many people. Everything is okay. We are always smiling.

"Do you find it hard to deal with passengers who have different customs and traits and speak differently?"

No, but sometimes, I just can't understand, and I go slow.

"Have you made friendships outside of the Filipino group and tried their foods?"

Yes, I have. Some from Burma and Indonesia. Most of the time I try Indian foods. Special curry. Especially spicy garlic. I like it, because my friend, before I came back here (on my second contract), is an Indian guy.

"Can you think of any nice passenger stories?"

Mostly just honor a passenger request, and make them happy.

"What do you like most about your job?"

Everything. I need to enjoy my job here on a ship. I don't want to get stressed, just enjoy.

"How long did it take to get adjusted, since you had never worked on a ship before. Didn't you go through some kind of culture shock?"

I guess maybe one to three months, because I missed my family, but now, I'm okay. The daily routine changed a lot, and it was hard before one month. Now, I'm totally adjusted. I share a room with a man from Mauritius.

"What's something that you brought with you from home that you just can't live without?"

Maybe my phone, because I need communication with my family. I call every night when I finish my duty around 11 o' clock in the evening.

"What's your favorite place when you got off the ship at a port?"

I think my favorite port is Norway.

Jordan about to serve a guest

CHAPTER THIRTY-SIX

🦅 *Galley Steward: Frezer Joseph Pereira: India*

I just like people

The kitchen or galley on Columbus buzzes with activity day and night in preparation for the thousands of meals that will fly up the escalators for hungry guests. A sanitized and healthy area is the beginning of the process of cooking.

This is my first contract here, but I was working with another company before. A galley supervisor supervises the dishwashing and pot washing.

"Do you find it hard, working with people from different cultures?"

Yes, because some of the guys, they have some problems, like language problems. They don't understand. We just try to speak with them. We find it's a little bit harder, but we can manage it.

"And did they have gestures that they use? Hand motions and some customs that are hard to deal with as well?"

Sometimes it's very hard to explain to them. Because, in different cultures, we have some different signs. But they understand. Everybody understands. When we try to speak with them most properly in English, they can learn some things. When they came here, they didn't know much about English.

"Do you have to write reports on what you do?'

We write reports about all the dish-washing machines and other wash machines. The logs are filled in, three times a day, with temperatures and information. We put it in the computer, and then we send it to the maintenance people if there is a problem with the machines. The next day they come and fix the problems.

"So how many dishwashers do you have that you're talking about?"

We are not washing manually. We put all the things in the machine.

We have two dishwashing machines and one pot washing machine on deck six plus more machines for the crew galley, and the Plantation Bistro.

So, eight dishwashers wash all the dishes that we use. Four people are standing in front, and four people stand in back.

The dish washing machine washes, washes them again, and then dries them. As soon as they're dry, they're all taken out, and then new ones are put in. They're just constantly in use except at night. They have gloves to protect their hands from heat. Even the pots are washed by machine. The big soup pots are washed manually. For the dough mixers in pastry department, we have three sinks, and one cleaning system, it's called "the three-sink system" or "three bucket system". So normally, when they clean the surface, like these tables and working areas, they use the three-bucket system. You wash with soap water, rinse with clear water, and sanitize with chlorine water. We use one chlorine tablet. It's a hundred PPM [Parts Per Million]. We have this PPE, or personal protective equipment, like the gloves they wear for this cleaning. When the crew uses chemicals, they have to use PPE like gloves, apron, goggles and/or a mask.

"How did you learn this job?"

I started with Aida in 2010 and was in galley utility and did three contracts and learned everything I know now, and then I was promoted to galley supervisor. Step by step.

"Do you have a roommate who shares your room?"

Because I am a supervisor, I have my own room and live alone. I'm not quite happy about that, because sometimes I feel so lonely. When you go to your cabin you just have to watch TV, and then you sleep.

My friends come to my cabin, and we talk, and that makes me happy. I can like everybody. I like to make friends from other countries as well.

"Do you ever travel to other countries when on vacation?"

I stay at home when my contract is finished, because my wife doesn't get her vacation at the same time. So, I want to spend more time with my family.

"Do you have a secret as to how you get along so well with people?"

Frezer: Plate covers are sterilized after each use

I just like people and to make new friendships.

"What would your advice be to a young person just coming on board ship about what they're going to experience? How would you suggest they approach getting along with other cultures?"

I don't know about the other people's ideas, but some of the people don't

Spotless kitchen

like to mix with other people. I cannot really say that about the people I can mix with. The guys are not going to exist with them unless they have the language. It's not easy to understand them. The language is a big issue. It's interesting.

"Do you have anyone on the ship that you look up to, or you would like to be more like him?"

I have one and that is the Sanitation Officer, and I would like to be like him, because I like his job, and of course I would get more salary with more responsibilities in more departments.

CHAPTER THIRTY-SEVEN

Assistant Galley Steward: Zin Min Tun: Myanmar

I practice English

I worked on a touring deck oat efore coming here   , so this is my second contract on this ship.

, Was it har for you to et use to workin with ifferent cultures¡ "
Yes, ecause on the eck oat I ha more free om.

Here we have to think more aout our work , an we are takin care of people. I i n't speak any En lish when I starte . Now that this is the secon contract, I can speak a little it more En lish. At first when my officer tol me to o somethin , I i n't know what he was sayin .

I learn from watchin movies an rea in ooks. My teacher from ack home writes me every ay an tells me to practice an rea .

My cain mates are oth from Myanmar , an we practice speakin En lish a lot. We share wor s we've hear urin the ay that we on't un erstan an help each other.

"What is your jo description?"
I supervise the cleaners. If they don't know what to do, they ask me. I mostly work at night. I remind the crew to wear their PPE (personal protection equipment).

"At mealtime do you only sit with crew from Myanmar?"
No, I sit with Indonesians, and we talk in English.

"Do you have a place in your dreams you'd like to visit?"
I always think of going to Italy and Amsterdam. I love that it is cold there.

"What aout the food here? Are you used to it yet?"
Sometimes, when I get homesick, I eat some of the food I rought with me from home, like dried fish and tea leaves.

"What do you miss aout your home life?"
I married my wife just a year ago. She works in a hotel with the pulic.

"If you could change jos what are your goals?"

I would like to e a artender. I know nothing aout how to mix drinks. I just want to learn. I have to learn etter English , ecause you are more in touch with the guests. So maye in a couple of years.

CHAPTER THIRTY-EIGHT

Spa: Sylwia Dorosckiesicz: Poland

They give us a chance to travel

I'm coming from Poland, and I'm working in the spa.

"Tell us some of the things you do during the day."

Days are different, as there are two kinds of days on board. During the sea day, we are just working from 12 hours straight with breaks, and sometimes we can just do what we need to do.

I can work a lot and hard, and the next day you have port days. On port days, we are just cleaning up doing this and that. Just trying to survive and rest. Catching up on sleeping and so on.

"On port days you can get off the ship if you want?"

Every port day, we have half time of a passenger's time off. During that half time, we have time to really properly clean and do everything that we need to do. We are off three hours, so enjoy two and a half, because we have to take a shower before.

We travel a lot. They give us a chance to travel and go for excursions with guests. It's just nice from the cruise line. In two years, I have only missed two ports that I didn't get to see, because I was tired.

"Are you employees of the cruise line?"

We are a concession with a Greek company.

The English on board the ship is not really clear English; we call it ship language. We are using words from everywhere like Poland, Ukraine, India and Indonesia. You can go to another ship, and the crew knows the same language. I couldn't believe I was in the Caribbean Sea; later I was in Europe. My friends from school went to Australia. There's a lot of different cultures.

"Do you like the idea of working with many different cultures, or would you prefer that everybody was Polish?"

I know from times when I've been in Poland. I thought it's only one way of thinking, and I was thinking the same as every single one from my country; later on, I realized it's not healthy. There were a lot of rules. Now I'm coming back home, and I'm saying, no, don't think like that. It's not working, so go out from the rule. The ship, it's teaching how to treat people, how to understand people more. It's a good school for life. Maybe my son I will send, or my daughter. I don't know, because I don't have children yet.

I think it's easier to live with people when you know that your rules are, not from your home, but rules for all the world. You learn to treat people better, and you are not judged.

"Communication helps a relationship, because the people are really trying. There is an implication that you are going to help?"

It depends a lot on your personality, because I used to be the one who didn't talk or try to make friends. People would say you have a cell phone? Then write down what you want to say.

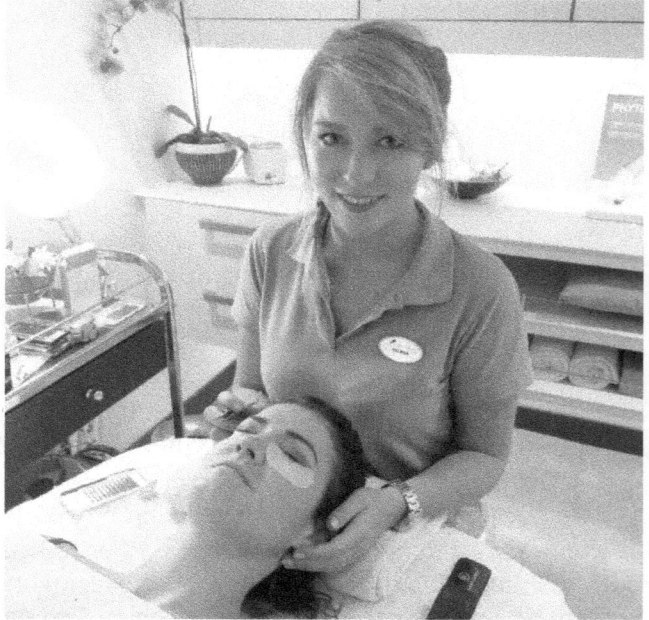

The Spa has many options

You are brave to catch this point or start to go into the group to hang out, or even to talk with passengers, just the small things. It's always in you. We have to just find the right people. Life is still beautiful.

"If people are missing their families, then you have something in common to bond with them?"

You can keep yourself busy so as to not think about that. But when you help people that are lonely, it's helping them to feel better.

CHAPTER THIRTY-NINE

🎁 *Spa: Sophia Rabie: South Africa*

I know how to adapt in a difficult situation

The spa is a favorite place for the ladies to pamper themselves. So now, all the crew memers will know their secret ways to keep the guests happy. Here is sustantially the conversation aout this operation aoard.

, Do you think there are a vanta es in all the ifferent cultures in the cultural iversity ein on oar ¡"

I efinitely think so. I think if you row up, you shoul not have only one set of i eas of, say the perspectives aout what's ri ht or what's wron ; or what wor s are hauntin , especially how to treat people. If I think aout it, it opens your min to see how other people o thin s, an what's etter or what's worse. For example, in this spa, especially, we have a lot of Serians now, an it's een very interestin to see. I knew them as personal in ivi uals efore this cruise, an now they roup to ether. So as personal in ivi uals, I've sometimes thou ht they were very irect people.

I realize that it's actually just a part of their culture, so it chan es my min to maye not always e so sensitive , or not to feel offen e or whatever. Now I coul just take it as it comes, an it really chan e my way of un erstan in how you can take thin s; you have to rea people in a ifferent way.

"How does it feel working with strangers a lot and always having to smile?"

I think it depends a lot on your personality. Some people can manage it, and some people cannot manage it. I think if you are coming to the ship, and having to do that. Because you are in pulic service, a perspective is very important for you as a person, ecause you're not always oin to e in a place that's easy, or you are ealin with people only when you feel like it.

I see people from the engine room or from the deck departments where they don't have to handle passengers or interact with passengers; life on oard is completely different from us, who have to deal with passengers; we have to e friendly and always happy and always welcoming. However, it's nice in the same reath , ecause we get a lot from passengers. So even if you're tryin to put up a face, an you look happy, people respon very well to that, an then you can also take that experience an roa en it.

Sylvia is one of the iggest reasons why I came ack on the ship to do another contract, ecause we got along so well during the previous contract.

We share a room together as well. If you've had a ad day , or you really don't feel like it, you know, there's someone who's also had a short night's sleep, or someone who has a sense of humor, so they can pick you up with a joke. That helps a lot, I think. I don't know if everyone has it, ut it's something that I would say makes it worthwhile, even if you're having a ad day or one that's not so easy.

"And what aout the customers relating to you? You're in a usiness where you spend more time with the customers in a more personal way. Do they relate to you more than their cain steward or waiter?"

I think it depends on the guests. Some guests, yes. Sylvia will say we talk a lot, so I think our English is a little it helpful there. We'll get to know more of a person. I think they relate more to us who are in a more intimate environment where the people come to relax, and to experience physical touch. You address things that they've een holding ack , or carrying on their shoulders for so long. It's actually a very nice area to work in.

"You're almost like a counselor, aren't you?"

In a way. Yes. I've heard some interesting stories. People might share the drama etween dinner companions, and it's really not like gossip.

Getting ready for the guests

More like a TV series, with little intrigues everywhere. You hear the different perspectives.

"Can you think of any random acts of kindness? People doing nice things for other people or etween the guests?"

Salvador Dali, a famous artist, regularly frequented cruise ships with his pet ocelot, Babou.

For sure etween the crew. I've had that a few times. We have to do laundry, right? Our own laundry. When you are off work and finished at nine, you're tired; you know you need to do laundry. You try to slip away in the day; you're good to go alone. A laundry cycle takes an hour. Often an hour goes y; you're dreading to go to put it from the washer to the dryer; a few times it's happened where it's een four or five hours, and I'm thinking everything is going to smell like dogs. And then I get to the laundromat; someone has just decided they're going to put all my clothes in the dryer, and the dryer is finishing, my duds are dry, and I am happy. Sometimes you cannot o to lunch, ecause you're workin too much or whatever. Someone will rin you a san wich; it's very nice. People make a point to reet you or say Bon Appetit.

"You are really like a family?"

Yes, and not everyone. I think the groups that stick together are more ecause of nationalities, not the department where you work. You just feel comfortale with people who speak your own language. People do mingle and spend time with other cultures.

, Suppose you ha a chance to talk to someo y who just came aoar in any capacity. What kin of a vice woul you ive them aout multicultural situations¡ How to act¡ "

It woul   epen where the person comes from. If it's someone who actually is from a nationality that's alrea y on oar , I woul think they woul n't have too many prolems slottin into a roup that alrea y speaks their lan ua e, or knows their culture. If it's someone coming from a completely different or unusual nationality, it depends. You have so little time to invest in someone. That is why random acts of kindness are so easy. It is easier when it's something small and something quick for you to do. People's schedules are different. Their eating times are different. Unless you live with someone, you don't spend that much time getting to know that person. If I had to give someone advice, I would say find someone in your department that you can connect with, ecause your working hours are the iggest chunk of your day. Make an effort to join a group, like a tale tennis competition. There are people on oard who speak little English , ut they are not in a guest area , so it's not a strict requirement. It is hard to reach out to them. The only way to improve in En lish is to use it. An for some people it epen s on why they are here, maye to travel or improve their positions.

"What would you do if you had a guest that was really angry, and was complaining, and you really didn't want to hear it?"

I think it depends on why they're complaining. If it's something that's got some truth ehind it, we need to address it. Do we need to figure out that this person is a complainer? Maye it is in their personality , and we can sort it out if we can. If you take it too personally, you'll just ruin your whole day. Then I will redirect it to my manager. She needs to deal with that.

"Anything in your personality that is magic which helps you get along with people?"

A person who ot me on the ship tol me to come on the ship, ecause he sai you have the ri ht personality for the ship. I think I'm a very open-min e person. I'm a very frien ly person. I know how to a apt in a ifficult situation. That makes a ifference. Plus, I love to travel, an any cons are out-wei he y the pros.

We made a ucket list for the World Cruise. After work you just don't want to go to sleep. On our list are things like we want to have a ridge excursion, an engine excursion, take a picture with our flags everywhere, and to ride a camel. On our wall we have the itinerary and our thirty things on our ucket list.

CHAPTER FORTY

🎁 *Cabin Steward: Sura Astra I Nyoman: Bali*

The culture of all things is in us

Folks on a long cruise get very used to someone cleaning up after them, making eds, refreshing the athroom, etc. The guests will appreciate these stewards when they arrive home without their est crew friend.

We're asking questions of the crew to learn aout how different cultures work together.

"We will summarize your comments and hope they will e helpful to oth new and experienced crew memers. What are your ideas?"

I am a cain stewar from Bal i. We just nee to respect each other, for the culture of all thin s is represente in each human ein .

, Are there times when a uest others you or asks stran e questions¡ "

On a worl cruise it is ifferent, ecause we et to know the uest, an we are with them for four months. They on't other us , ut they share their oo an a situations. They mi ht share what happene on the shore that ay. My uests now like to share all their cruise experiences, an I really like to listen.

"What motivates you, when you are really tired, to get the jo done?"

It's not really hard work if you go y the rules. I have to service the rooms twice a day, ut I have time to take a rest in etween. Sometimes guests say, *"It is okay; please don't clean my room tonight."* I always tell them it is no prolem and not difficult for me , and I have plenty of time.

"When you have a guest who is angry, do you just go slow and show patience?"

To e a good crew memer, we have to e ale to explain our duties , so we oth understand them. The characteristics of the younger guests is very different from the older guests. You have to know with experience how to cool them down and talk with them.

First of all, we need to e ale to explain to the guests when they ask questions, like what is this or that. We like close communication.

"Aout how often do you change the sheets in the room?"

We have to change every four days. If I see something soiled, like a spot or leeding or whatever, if it is in the ed, then I have to change.

"Do you know how long the sheets last?"

Originally, we have the inventory. It's whatever the sheet looks like, so sheets last aout four months. Then , they have to replace them.

"Are there any things in the laundry that are pressed or ironed?"

They have a ig mangle, like a pressing machine for the sheets. The pillow cases: they go through the mangle.

"Do you know how many towels they wash in a day?"

It depends on the temperature outside. Now, going through the hot Asian countries, people take two showers a day.

, Do you like all the ifferent cultures aoar the ship¡ "

We learn from each other.

, I'm curious, when you hear aout the customs of other places to see , what it's like where they live, woul you love to o visit them¡ "

I have a frien livin in Darwin, so we met in the city an ha a oo time seein each other.

, When you have lunch or meal times, o you always sit with someone from Bali¡ "

Some from Myanmar an some others. From what I see, most people like to share with other nationalities.

, As crew memers you always protect an take care of each other¡ "

Yes, ut sometimes there is an er or a wor s sai , an the ship has zero tolerance for that type of ehavior. I have learne , as I et ol er, just to cool own.

"You have learned this from working on ships plus it is part of your culture isn't it?"

Yes.

We celerate our holidays with special

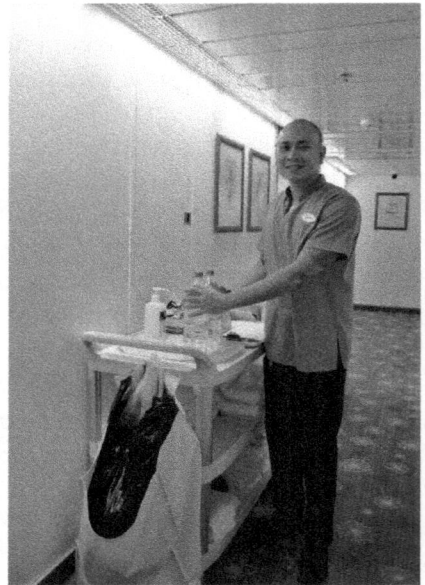

Nyoman Cabin Steward

foods, decorations, and invite everyone to enjoy with us.

"What kind of food do you miss from home?"

I am always calling my mom. My favorite dish is a fish dish made with onions and a spicy paste we call Samal. This is the first thing I request from my mother when I go home.

CHAPTER FORTY-ONE

🎁 *HK Jolly: Jewel Nevis Rocha: India*

Happiness is contagious

This is my 16th year. I started my career at age of 21. It was a surprise for me on my 21st irthday; I got a call from a cargo ship, and then I started my shipping life.

My responsiility on the ship is working in the housekeeping department. I am a jolly [runner]. I'm responsile to take care of a passenger's request or any other need, whatever they request. If they are not happy with the cain, I go and check around. If there is some prolem, I report it, ecause the reception is the one who is going to send me over there to check for it. For the safe ox, if it works to open, I teach the passenger how to use the safe walls to change the attery or to replace the safe. If there is no light or air in the ceiling, I do that. I check, and if there is a noise in the room, I inform them what kind of noise, and then they give this jo to another department.

"What are some strange things guests have asked you to do?"

Some of the strange things are looking for a noise which was outside of the ship. We have to track this prolem and speak to them so that they understand very well. We have to keep them happy. If they're having some prolem, we don't say that we cannot do it.

Our jo is to say that we can do it. Because they are coming for a holiday, and they spend money for this cruise, every single penny counts. When they spend money, we have to give something more, so the company name shines.

"What are some of the silly stories passengers have come up with? Like some passenger thought the safe was a microwave, and they wanted to know how to make it work?"

In my experience here was nothing like this, ecause the passengers are used to most things in their cain. Even at home , people are used to these things. Everything is changing. Life is changing. I do find it funny when they ask if the mini ar is chargeale , or is it free? I show them the list of prices, and later the Cain Steward will take inventory of refrigerator consumpti on, and the ship will charge the room.

Another thing that happens, even to the crew, is whenever you come off of the elevator, you're doing OK, ut they don't know whether they are in forward or aft. So, they ask me where is the gangway, and I tell them straight forward, and they start off. I have to go around ehind them and tell them , no you are going the wrong way. Passengers are very smart, and it doesn't take long to help them.

"You have to e happy and friendly and positive. Where do you get your motivation?"

If your family has given you these kinds of tips, like from your mother, your father has taught you how to respect people, and when you have a good family, you're very friendly.

The frien liness comes with how you choose your frien s. If you rew up with oo frien s, nei hors an society, then you will e the same on oar ecause you live here.

Aboard the World War 2 British battleship HMS Vanguard, an Engineer traveled 7 miles and climbed 3,000 feet of stairs daily during his turn of inspection, and the ship's bakery produced 1,000 lbs. of bread daily.

I work, maye it's seven months, eight months, nine months. So that means I'm more into the sea life than my own home or vacation, which is for three months. They say you are just like a tourist at home; just come relax, and sleep on a ed, and food is prepared for you.

The passen ers pass y where we are workin . So, we have to e always smilin . There are ups an owns in our family as well. It's like we have to collaorate with each other. Each an every prolem nee s to e solve . It's the same thin over here.

We are as a family. You have to stay to ether an live to ether. We share a same mess room, the crew memers, an everythin . We eat to ether, we make jokes, we make fun. A lot of times, we share with each other the sa ness an oo times an the est ays. I norin someone is like killin someone's life an happiness. For me, I'll just ive my est, an with a smile, even if I'm scare , I'm not showin it to anyone. A etter smile is a etter ay. I think so in my life.

I learned a lot of things from my school days. I had good teachers who have now passed away. Mostly my parents and grandparents have taught me the right way. I never give up and always focus.

"When people have a prolem , do they tend to turn to those in their own culture?"

In India, we don't have a culture prolem or a caste prolem. I am used to it; we never discriminate against anyody, for example, like in former days under the caste system. In the olden days yes, ut now the young generation is all united.

"Have you had someone come from Myanmar or someplace else to you for counseling and help?"

I always help. Most of the people from Myanmar are having some need and also from Ukraine. They have a prolem with the English and have miscommunications. But, whenever they ask me, I just tell them very clearly so that they can understand it, and do their things properly. Whatever you do, you have to do it in a positive way.

We are very lucky in India, ecause we got this language to study from our childhood. I am not saying that some are not qualified, as they are very qualified. It's just their English needs help. If you know something you cannot hide it. You have to teach someone. Learning never stops, my grandfather used to say.

"Have you ever had to train someone for your own jo , ecause you are moving into a new department?"

Yes, when I worked for Costa, I worked in the engine room as a wiper. A wiper cleans everything in the engine room to make it clean. I had to cross-train someone from the galley. I was going home in two months, and he was replacing me, and I had to make him ready. If he had an accident, then maye he could say that I never taught him. It was really tough for me, ecause he was not asoring this in his rain   , ecause it was not his profession. The engine room is very noisy, so it was hard to communicate, and is not like we do it now. We wear ear plugs now. He is still working for that company, and he always texts me and tells me how I did such a good jo of training him. Because of you I am someone else. I'm happy. The thing is if I keep myself happy, I like to focus on people who are ivin a oo example for this worl . Happiness is conta ious. If you are not happy, that means you are makin a mistake in your life. Whatever the sa ness is, the oo an the a come like the ti e in the water. You cannot expect the ti e will e just at that level, so sometimes it will e hi her. Sometimes we ca n have a isaster in one villa e so you have to always e prepare for this kin of a thin , oth lower an hi h ti es.

"Do you think the experience of eing in the crew is lifting people up a little it? Do they feel like they're making progress in their life?"

I can only guess that they are doing this, ut I don't know what is happening with other human things. If they take it positive, and they elieve they are doing something good, and they are happy with it, and trying to improve, and make something e tter y tomorrow, definitely they will e happier in their profession. This is not only the company telling us this. It must come from the heart. You can see the artificial smiles, and you can see the natural smile, ecause we are human. So, you just smile like this, and the next time they can see you are not happy. You must not pretend, as it's a ig mistake. So, if you are sad, then you show you are sad, and you try and work it out with smiles.

Sometimes I sit with the mixed tales, you know, sometimes t here are our own people from Goa. I don't have any prolem . I follow all cultures an all the reli ions. I try everyo y's kin of foo , whatever it is. If I on't like it, I on't eat it.

My ancestors were all sailors. My grandfather and father explored the world. The thing is, it's in our roots. Who has money to see the worl ¡ Even if you trie to walk aroun the worl you woul never finish it.

You cannot keep your ol footprints on all parts of the worl , you know. We just work for it. So, it's a good advantage to ecome a sailor. If you get free

A "jolly" with a mission

time, you are here in Australia and can take a picture of their houses, and I keep it for the memories. This is a ig souvenir for you. I used to plan to see places like the Taj Mahal, ut I stopped planning and take each day at a time.

"Do you have some thoughts that you'd like to pass on to other people through the eBook?"

Whenever you work for the company, you have to e a very responsile person to rin this company up with ri htness. You know, this company will row much etter. We have to ive solutions; we have to ive our i eas.

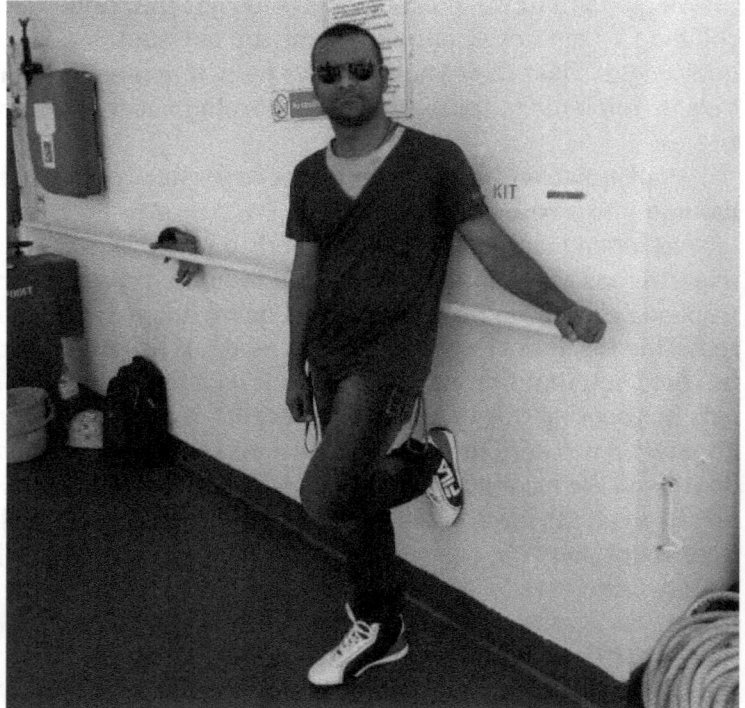

The company shoul have oo i eas, e cause we come from ifferent countries.

We on't nee to make a copy an paste from other companies. My mother always use to say, *"Don't follow the guy who is going the other way"*. You choose your way, which is etter for you.

Passing through the Suez Canal

Follow what the main office tells us to do. We are following a leader here. That's why they are happy with us. They say we can uy new ships; we can give jos for the othe r guys who are waiting at home. There are many people in my country. They are waitin for a small jo on the ship or anywhere else, ecause they nee lea ers like us to e ale to rin them alon .

I wante to su   est it. You know I am there for the crew after meetin s I
o to. I represent them. I o for the safety meetin , so I ive my su   estions
for them an   pass it to the company. I"m reamin not only aout myself in
the picture, ut I"m reamin for who is lookin out for the jo. So, if we
helpe this company in a etter way, the etter the future will ecome.

I"m very happy with this company. If there are 600 crew memers here,
they were joless at home. Now they"re taken y the CMV. I am very prou
for this owner. He was just like a crew meme r. This owner, he has a i
vision. When we are orn, we come with zero sense. Everythin comes from
our mother an father. Once we start learnin , that is our first step. When I
first met the owner, he was like a crew memer, very frien ly. All of the
o sses are frien ly an helpful, askin questions an   what are the
prolems. I feel like I am at home here.

CHAPTER FORTY-TWO

Lighting/ Sound Technician: Eric Monday: Philippines

Frosting on performance cake

Eric is a professional with sound and lighting and responsible for the frosting on the performance cake.

We can summarize his words by pointing to his commitment to be a reliable partner with the performers when he says that he's a sound and lights technician.

We do set ups for any party. We sometimes are a DJ, and we set up all the production shows and the guest shows, and then also we do a maintenance on old equipment: lights, really.

This is my first contract, but with another company, I was working in Australia. I was there for three years while I was with P. and O.

I have been a sound technician for radio stations. I made commercials for radio my first time. I wanted to work at a cruise line. When I first came on board in my previous company, I thought I would just sit in an office, because it's production, but it's different.

I never knew how to set up things like a whole band. Before, I made commercials for radio and jingles for politicians. On the ship, it was different. They put me backstage working with the cast, and I never worked like that before. So, it was crazy.

I was a mass communications student, and I'm also a journalist. That's why I was in radio, because in my school, we had this tri-media radio broadcast. So that's why I went to radio.

My boss is the cruise director in the entertainment

Let the light and sound begin

department. When I first came, I wanted to see different people, like different races.

I see the world is like the cultural diversity on the ship.

When you're on the ship, everybody thinks you speak English very well. On the ship you can see different kinds of people, and you can see the world.

Vladimir and Eric are a creative lighting team

CHAPTER FORTY-THREE

Head Pastry Chef: Neil Fernandes: India

CMV gives freedom to grow

Occasionally we come across people with a true "passion" for their jo. The following paraphrased story speaks for itself.

"What do you like most aout your jo?"

I can't say it in words; it just makes me feel who I am when I do my stuff. I have no words to say. I just love it. Nothing can stop me.

"You are really creative in your jo. That's part of who you are, right?"

This jo lets you express yourself. Ima ination is what comes to my min . I can create anythin at the moment. Noo y

Neil adding the finishing touch to desserts

ju es you; you can use your own i eas. We o have the company's stan ar recipes. We have to follow those. But, when we have some uffets, you can use your own ima ination.

"What's the funniest thing that has happened etween you and guests?"

I don't recollect; ut normally it would e, when I do some stage shows for a unch of guests, some things don't turn out right. So that's th e time I need to play around and try out things.

I started when I was 21. That was on Celerity Cruises. It's een aout 16 years.

"Do you think there are advantages to the cultural diversity on the ship?"

Yes, ecause I have learned a lot from different n ationalities. These days with all the different cultures, we can mix the food traditions.

I"m in the foo in ustry; I really enjoy the foo from ifferent nationalities, especially Ukraine, Russia, In onesia, an I also enjoy the people an the frien ly amiance. It"s really very nice. I min le less with my own nationality. I look for other nationalities.

"You mentioned Ukraine. What aout their food? Is it sweet or sour?"

Ukraine cooking has nothing to do with curry. It's totally different. It's very nice. It's more on the savory side, ut it's more with meats; it's more pasta, and it's really nice.

"Are there things aout the ship life that you miss when you go home?"

Yes, ecause most of your time is spent on oard so it's like eing with your family. Even when I am leaving the ship, there are tears in my eyes. You keep thinking when you are home, what is going on there, and is everything right? It's really hard sometimes. So, you miss the people.

What o you think you"ve learne from workin on the shipį

I i learn a lot. Goo an a , to e unselfish as well. That"s the first thin , I think, ecause I wasn"t like this when I first joine the ship.

The best chefs on the ocean

, What o you mean y ein unselfishį "

People are just sometimes crew memers. It"s a ive an take policy. If you ive your oo , the ay you stop, you want; it's like that. You"ve learne to e unselfish. I wasn"t like this efore. I"ve learne a lot that is interestin .

"What do you think your greatest strength is?"

My will power. Nothing can stop me. Even if I have to wake up in the morning at two for a jo, I'm ready for it.

"You work in this fast-paced environment?"

I love it. Every moment there is something to do. Yes, I had to learn.

"You carry two tools on your sleeve pocket?"

I have tools on my sleeve; a pen is a necessity; it's very important. And I have a highlighter. That's so my guys don't miss something. I focus them on the recipes or any of the menus, or what's going to e done. I just highlight all this stuff.

, What o you think your secret is in ettin alon so well with people¡ "

I think it's my kin ness. I'm a type of person to ive away thin s. I have a i heart. My assistants love workin with me. They miss me when they're on the other ships.

"What makes this cruise line a little different?"

I have never felt our ships were like a cruise liner; I just feel when I'm comin ack , it's like home; then when I see the same uests, it's really eautiful. When they know you an you know them, it's like an attachment.

> Sailors tell spooky legends about mysterious ships that roam the seas with no one aboard for decades. The Russian cruise ship Lyubov Orlova broke free from a tugboat in 2013 and is now contentedly floating around the North Atlantic.

We don't have a lot of pressure over here compared to the other cruise lines. Mental stress isn't there, so you're freer to work.

Aout 90% of our guests give good comments, ecause they're always happy. I love to see the smiles when I go, even at the restaurant. I like to add those special drizzles and things for desserts. I show the first sample. Then I show it to my guys, and then they carry on. Some days I let the crew e creative.

, Do you fin the customs of all these cultures har to eal with¡ "

I have een on oar for so many years that I know which people like what , an how to eal with ifferent nationalities. It's no prolem at all. I just ju e everyo y the same way . As lon as they coul e oo with me , then I am oo with them.

, An estures from other cultures you just et use to¡ "

Yes, we o it quite often. Like when you are in Jamaica, you alrea y know some stuff. We even use them at home with frien s. It's silly, ut it ets into your enes, I uess.

"Who is the wisest person you've met?"

The wisest person I know is my teacher, and he's my mentor. That was my pastry chef. He's not on oard. In the hotel industry, he was the one to really ring me up to this. I'm almost like him. He's in the UK.

He came with his family last year and spent the day with me. It was very touching. I met him after 10 years. It was very nice. So, it was even exciting for him. He was proud, of course.

I got my creativity from my mother. We used to always do Christmas sweets and puddings. Both my parents were really interested in this. So that's where I really started a liking for this.

"Do you get ored with cooking the same things over and over?"
No, I try my est every time to do something much etter than the previous dessert. Though the recipe is the same, everything will e a little it touchier in there. You can still make a ig difference.

"What do you do with leftovers? How do you know how much food to prepare?"

Like now, for the world cruise, we are eating in the Bistro. So, we have an approximate count. So, we

> The largest cruise ship in the world burns 11361 gallons of fuel each hour or 12 feet per gallon.

don't over prepare for the first seating. Once it's gone to the tale , it cannot go ack. So, it goes to the garage. If it has een refrigerated   , then it can go to the crew memers.

"If you run out for the first seating, you really have to e quick and know the ingredients."

With meats, you cannot cook them ahead and keep them, so they have to e fresh as well. The vegetales also have to e done precisely from the freezer to cooking.

"Do you ever run out of food, like in first seating? What do you do?"

We seldom run out of food. It happened to me maye twice. I don't allow that chance. Maye I would prepare a little more, ut when it happens, then I have to use my rain logic. Something to really cope with. So that's the specialty of a chef as well. You do a trick and e smart enough. But the guests don't know aout it.

"Do you have a favorite person on oard who you like to share your thoughts with?"

I have a good friend on oard named Olga from Ukraine . We communicate very well and understand each other. We spent almost five years together on Marco Polo. She was there with me. She's the closest one. She has een to my city as well as to my home.

"Is it hard to train new people when they are from a different nationality than yours?"

As long as I can see the person really wants to learn, then it is easier. If a person shows his interest, I can feel it. When I first communicate with a new crew memer, I show them around once or twice. They really get comfortale when they pick up things easily.

"From the human relations side, what is most important to share with someone new coming aoard?"

They have to e strong. It's not just ecause of the ship's motions. It's the amiance. You're going to e away from home, and you will miss that If you have the willpower that you really want to grow up in life; if you really want to see the world, that's helpful.

"Is there room for promotion?"

Previously we just had two ships. Now, when we are growing, there are a lot of people getting promoted. A lot of good chances. You can even change the department, if you really aren't happy with what you're doing here. You could change y cross

> *Why are the ruins in such bad condition?*

training, so a lot of good opportunities. The head of the department counsels people. He is going to look at your evaluation and see if you have interest. I have people I am proud of and am watching.

Last year, there was one uy who was very intereste in pastries. He use to come after hours an work with me, pickin up hints. He alrea y has een promote in the same contract. It was very touchin for me. He is a aker now , an I can see that smile on his face, an he loves what he is oin . I am prou of myself, an my assistant wants to e a pastry chef. So, it's like someo y rou ht me up , so now I am oin my est to rin someone else up.

"So, for fun, sounds like you are the life of the party?"

I love music. Especially Latin music even though I am Indian. Yes. I love it, ecause I picked it up more from the other cruise line. Most of t hem really think that I am Latino as well. I was in hiding! People want to dance with me. I just dance with everyody. It doesn't matter to me. As long as I can dance as well.

"So, during the week, if there is no crew party do you go to your room?"

I go to the crew ar and relax and have a chat, listen to some music. I go to the gym often for an hour of exercise.

"How do you stay so thin, eing a pastry chef?"

Being a pastry chef and staying thin is in the family genes; we are all like this. My mom, she's the est person in my life. She's een my est friend, my est teacher. Both my parents. She stayed with me the last year on oard two days. She is coming on aoard ag   ain in Cochin to Mumai. She gets really excited when she talks aout me. She is so proud. I do have an elder rother and a younger sister. They are oth   settled. I have a wife at home. I have my son 11 years in fourth grade. I use Messenger to

Artistry on a plate

communicate with them quite often.

CHAPTER FORTY-FOUR

❀ *Bartender-Coffee Barista: Made Diwa: Bali*

Smile: it doesn't cost anything

Everyone makes coffee at home. Did you realize there was so much "science" ehind that hot cup of jo? This interview sheds light on a creative and friendly crew memer's jo and attitudes.

I'm from Bali, Indonesia, near the city center and was orn in 198 7 in a place almost like a forest. My father and mother helped us growing up to learn and survive in life, ut y the time I was nine years old, when I was in elementary school, they agreed to separate. I don't understand yet aout the reason. I was left alone until some family came and picked me up to live with them. They taught me everything aout life. I learned how to save money to pay for school.

"Tell us aout your jo?"

My jo is the est choice for me. My experience on land was artending.   The hospitality in ustry is aout service. Everythin is international. I worke with another company efore, a Spanish company, an I was learnin Spanish lan ua e. Then I trie to et a jo on a loal cruise line, last year, on Columus. I starte as an assistan t arten er. I starte to learn more how to stan out, ecause ifferent companies have ifferent rules. Then I ot a promotion from my supervisor. They recommen e me to e a ar mana er. They approved a promotion. I learned another skill which interests me. It's aout coffee.

When I started to work, noody knew the way the coffee maker worked. Day y day, I like d to learn. Then I saw some videos, and I learned from the Internet, and I saw how the masters make coffee, and then, every day, I try to learn. I feel like now I have something extra from my side. Everyody can e a artender and make cocktails , ut not everyody can e a coffee arista. So, this is the plus point I like. Then I got a lot of comments from the guests.

"You speak three languages then, English, Indonesian and Spanish?"

I can speak a few words if I met some Spanish people. But with languages, you need practice ecause you forget , if you don't use it. I can write Russian, ut I cannot speak it. English is not my mother language, ut I like to speak English, and I like to work with the guests. The Australian English I can understand, ut the English spoken from the UK is more diffic ult for me, and I have to listen closely.

"Are your friends here just from Bali?"

I have a lot of frien s here from Ukraine. Also, from UK, In ia, Myanmar, Belarus, an some ancers from Ukraine an a lot of other nationalities. The speakin is always ifferent, ecause they have a ifferent culture, ifferent accent. It is nice to work with a lot of nationalities. We know ifferent cultures, ifferent lan ua es.

Sometimes it mi ht soun like they are speakin ru ely, or they think I am not speakin well. But it's not true, it's just the ifference in the lan ua e. We

Mariners often carried cages of crows for use in coastal navigation. If uncertain to the bearing to nearby lands they would release one of the birds who would usually fly in the shortest most direct route to land. The term as the crow flies has come to mean the most direct route between two points.

will un erstan how they mana e, how they live in their home, in their country, ecause we will see an example. It's how to work, how to live. Examples are Seria or Ukraine. When we have een on oar a while, they will e talkin aout each an coconut, an I say to them that I have a lot of each an a l ot of coconut, so we will talk aout our cities. This is ifferent, ut it makes us happy. We know a lot of kin s of foo , so from In onesia, or Ukraine, there is always ifferent foo .

We can try new ones, including those from India. Ukrainian soup, at least we can try, and we all have different tastes, ut at least we know. This is ship life. You egin to know more things ; at least when you go on vacation or when we have finished work on the ship, we can share with the young people.

"You see a lot of strangers each day. How do you keep up your good attitude and smiling?"

For me, smilin is like my personality. If you are an ry or hurt, you shoul never show to the outsi e.

The thin is to smile; it oesn't cost anythin . No matter how ru e the passen er, how complainin the passen er, we serve with a smile. They will calm own, an they will e very happy.

This is not special foo we serve here, ut if we serve with special service an with a smile with our heart, they think it is special. If we on't have passen ers, then we on't have a jo. So, we nee to ive them the est service, so they will come ack a ain.

"What is the hardest part of your jo."

I didn't see any hard work from my jo, to e honest   , ecause I love it. If the coffee is not hot, they will send it ack.   It's all aout patience. If you are   not patient, you will think it is hard. But from my side it's very easy.

We do alcohol, we do coffee, everything. The thing is, they put me in a coffee shop as usual. They like what I do; they put me there, ut if they want me in a ar as well, I can do that, ecause, for me   , in the pulic ar or the alcohol ar, it's easier f or me.

Maye when the passenger sees this is a coffee ar, they might not realize it, ut I have also cocktails , or whatever, plus all the cookies.

Made, Barista, with his smile

CHAPTER FORTY-FIVE

🎁 *Bar Waiter: Irina Ruticov: Romania*

I had three dreams

A ar waiter is almost invisile to the guest, until they are needed, and then they magically appear to help the process of ringing whatever is needed to your hands. The following summarizes some questions and answers from the perspective of a ar waiter.

, Do you think there are a vanta es to the cultural iversity on the ship¡ "

Everyo y's ifferent. This has helpe me un erstan a lot aout the people from Ukraine, Hon uras or In ia. It epen s also on the country. They're havin a ifferent kin of foo . I was tryin , most of them, the In ian, the Hon uras, the Ukrainian; it's almost similar with mine. I think it ets pretty nice to meet other people from another country. That is, they are oin to open your min more.

"Do you have prole ms with customs and traits from other cultures?"

No. I am on duty, and sometimes all of us, we are tired, and all of us, we are having hard days, good days, fun with each other. I do not like to lame the country, so if the person is a it tired, or I'm a it tired, he doesn't have to consider my country or my nationality. I don't think that it has to do with the country they come from.

"And tell us what your jo is. What do you do?"

I'm a waitress. I'm serving drinks for the people who would love to drink. It's pretty nice. Before, I didn't have any idea aout what are all the spirits or vodka or gin. I didn't have any, ecause in my country I have a different kind of alcohol. The people, when they are having a glass of wine, share stories.

"What's it like working with strangers, and you have to smile and e well?"

There is always a way forward, so you just have to meet them. They will not e strangers any more.

"What do you like most aout your jo?"

You just have to find, in yourself, okay today is another day, and I'm going to find something new. Maye I'm oin to have a new conversation, an I like to speak with the people. I learn a lot of thin s from the passen ers, from the places where they come from.

And if I did the comparison etween my country and then yours, if you're from England or America. All right. I have to speak with you. I am a very curious person. I like to travel. My parents did not travel. Only my father once,

when he was working in Turkey. I am working for a house or a car, ut I
have to stop when I cross the limit. I don't need so much.

I woul like to travel also, when I'm at the proper a e for my ki s.
Because some people, for example, in my country, they're workin their
entire life to have one, two cars, two houses, one apartment, ut actually
they on't fin their
happiness there. The people
comin on the ship are
happy. They visit a lot of

> There are more than 2,000 ports
> which can be visited by cruise ships.

places. That's a very mature attitu e. It really helps. But to e honest , on
the ship, it's really nice to meet another kin of person.

You have an open mind. You know a few words from each language. I
want to say yes. When you are meeting a new programmer, who is on the
ship, on his first contract, I want to know how to say hello in his lan ua e
or thank you. It makes him happy that he is here, an these people that
know my lan ua e are nice. It makes us oth comforta le.

"What makes you so out-going and motivates you?"

This is my third contract. In my first one, it was a it harder, ecause I
didn't know what I had to do. I didn't know how to approach people. Also,
the country matters; I'm not alone on the ship. My oyfriend is here. That
makes me feel etter when I'm with him, and the things are easier when
you finish working. He has listened to me. A good friend can do that. Just to
share the story with someone. You trust all these things. Believe me, that
communication can help very much.

"When you go home, are there things aout the ship life that yo u miss?"

Oh yes. Going outside with my friends, and making ad jokes etween
us. If I'm visiting at home for two months, It's not aout the money. When
I'm at home, and I have already enough days, that makes me feel ready to
come ack and start on another contract. It's much easier when I know my
friends are with me.

"Do you know anything aout how to talk with someody from a
completely different culture?"

Well, for example, yesterday, I was havin a conversation with a uy. I
am very intereste aout th e o s from Hin u reli ion. Some of them
involve the elephants. I'm a reli ious person, ut when it's aout the
reli ion, I'm very curious, ecause my ui e tol me aout each culture
havin a o . I sai , just on't feel a that I am askin so many questions ,
ecause I just want to know more. When my collea ues ask me aout my
country, I just o on aout this an that. Come to visit me.

When you're at home and, let's say that also your friend is going home, we can visit each other. I was having a colleague from Seria who was also a very good friend with my oyfriend, and they are very close. I said, we are near Romania, and he said, okay, ecause he was having a vacation there aout 200 kilometers more to his place from mine.

I said, well if you will have time, we will e going there. It was nice. Unfortunately, we didn't have a lot of time, ut he offered that to us in the future. I also did this with a Brazilian, and it's nice.

"You put your finger on something when you said you wanted to know more aout the Hindu religion ; is that curiosity?"

Well, it's interesting. Then for example, on my previous ship, they were havin an elephant statue, an   each memer from the restaurant was lau hin an   ancin , an I aske what oes that mean. It was somethin aout the temple, an someone was explainin aout the culture, an   that was very interestin . My collea ue just tol me the Water Festival is comin up as well as the Color Festival in In ia. He showe me some won erful pictures. So, I ha questions like why is that festival aout colors¡ I am open to this kin of knowle e.

In the first month, when you are coming on the ship, you're a it scared, ecause proaly some people never speak English at home, day after day. After a month or two or three weeks, they're opening themselves up, ecause this is what's happening with me. We have to

Ship life brings us together

know each other. An   you have to know aout the reli ions, aout the festivals, or what is the most visite place in a country. An why not¡ On my vacation, I am oin to visit.

Trays of treats

The ship life rings us together, and we are still together , next vacation, to travel with each other.

I had three dreams aout travel. One was to see the northern lights. I've seen it with the ship. The second one is the Chinese wall. And the third is to visit America, and I know that they're going to happen.

CHAPTER FORTY-SIX

🦅 *Home Office-Development: Jakob Kummer: Austria*

All jobs are important

Jako is responsile within the Home Office in Athens for crew training and company development. He is a thoughtful, roadly -experienced person who has a vision for growth and a plan to take good care of the workers y meeting their immediate and long-term needs.

They are largely responsile for delivering the est cruise product possile to guests they hope will return each year. He has developed a useful system that involves a Crew Amassador who has regular meetings with department amassadors. These ga ther the legitimate needs and suggestions from crew memers; then he implements the ones that will enrich the lives of the crew after their work day is over.

Crews work continuously for seven days a week, ut they have time each day for enrichment, naps, and socialization with other crew memers at meals and other times. Some have contact with guests. The following information was provided in an interview with Jako while he was on oard the World Cruise on the Columus, flagship of CMV, [Cruise and Mariti me Voyages].

On cruise lines, the crew works for an agreed time, such as 8 months, non-stop, and then takes time off, for 2 or 3 months, to e with family or do other things such as education or travel. New crew memers are assigned a ship, arrive for their appointed start date, listen to a rief orientation, and tour the ship; they egin work that day with on -the-jo training in general assignments, such as hotel tasks in the restaurant or the cain steward area.

On the marine side, the new crew memers generally have experience and qualifications. The first month away from their home area can e challenging, and Jako has addressed improvements in helping new crew to e patient for at least a month, while adjusting to life away from home. Over time, the crew issues are dealt with through the amassador system. Jako's vision ali ns with all mana ement people in implementin an attitu e of respect, teamwork, an carin for every team memer.

Jako states that military service and ships are perhaps the last two ig industries in this world where leadership authority has to exist, ecause otherwise it would e difficult to handle emergencies. These ays, there is also a theme that involves how to treat people, how to respect each other, an how to work with a multicultural team. Jako a mits he is quite a fee ack machine. He ives constructive fee ack; an then he tries to explain to people on oar how mana ement supports them, an how each can support each other.

Jakob and Elian

So how does CMV work with this team, what is its work ethic, and how can all workers achieve more customer satisfaction?

For new crew, the first day is a challenge.

There is no time to look around to see how the ship is working. We have limited eds. That means if someody is leaving for vacation, and another one is taking over the ed and the station or the working area, there are not a lot of hours for hand-over time.

We have a longer hand-over time for the heads of departments, ecause they can't go over the whole department in an hour. For those people, of course, we have a few days' time. Work starts when entering the ship after the safety instruction, after the familiarization, and after we show them the ship's decks.

> *Edible gold leaf is the world's most expensive food. It sells for $15,000 USD per pound, and it is served on a Silver Sea cruise as the most expensive cruise ship meal decorating a creamy risotto.*

Jako thinks : It's a won erful thin to have a multi-cultural, multi-nationality, multi-character firm. The lan ua e is En lish.

The uys in the en ine room know that without servin foo an cleanin the cains, our four en ines own elow are useless. We woul not e   sailin any more. The reverse is true on the hotel si e.

This is the first thin , that we tell them: listen, all these jos on oar are important. This is from our mana ement point of view; I think that the clue is to ive all of our crew memers the fee lin that they're important, from the person who is oin the en ine control to the one who makes the e s.

The crew amassador arranges good parties. He goes to the crew sport contests. Two years ago, crew welfare was not as evident. Now he handles welfare on a regular asis and takes care of issues with crew food, and a long list of other things. He was mentioning the Bile group and the rain teaser contest.

We have the different classes and encourage the footall team and asketall team. Then we have   a Ukulele group and the raffles. He is taking care of cain issues and organizing the get -togethers with the shore excursion team.

We celerate the Indian National Day. Different nationalities have invite their frien s from Belarus an elsewhere. Maye it's ifferent reli ions, ifferent cultures, ifferent political orientations, an   ifferent nationalities. If you o to the crew area, people are sittin an talkin to ether at the In onesians' tale for lunch or inner , for example, an also sittin with their community, ecause it's easier for them to communicate.

Jako's mission is development. It's happening now.

CHAPTER FORTY-SEVEN

🎁 *Crew Ambassador: Joseph Mebin: India*

Nothing is impossible

"Happy crew makes happy guests." **What I do in a nutshell is exactly what a cruise ship director does for his passengers.** It's all entertainment, so that is what I do for the crew, because they spend 8 to 10 months on board the ship. That means they spend more time with us than they do with their families back home. So, my job is to entertain them, keep them busy, pursue their hobbies, if they have any, look into the food control, like the quality of the food, and monitor the accommodation areas. Any problems they face in terms of maintenance issues? They come to me. We have a system in the computer called AVO which stands for Avoid Verbal Orders, and it defines the deficiencies of the cabin, and who is in charge of that. We monitor that as it has to be resolved in the next 24 hours. And I keep on checking till these things are done in a timely manner.

We have 650 crew members living in 400 cabins, so there are always maintenance issues. We also offer a kind of counseling and advice if the crew member has any problem personally, or work related, and I am the first person they come to see. I have my office hours posted (10:00AM-12:00AM), so they know when they can see me, and I carry a beeper and a radio. I am available 24/7 in case of urgent matters.

To entertain them, we offer bingo games, raffles, crew parties, team nights, sports fests (including four to five indoor games like chess, darts, pool table, foosball and table tennis) and two outdoor games (basketball and football if available in a port). I usually contact the port agent well in advance and ask a few standard questions, like is there free Wi-Fi available in the terminal? If not, where is the nearest Wi-Fi available so the crew members can get in touch with their families. I ask where the

Joseph Mebin

nearest shopping mall is for them to buy toiletries, and the third question is always if there is an available football or basketball court which is a walkable distance from the ship?

Asia and Pacific Plaza, Shanghai Science Museum station, Subway Line No.2. Is one shopping area with all under one roof? Eateries, electronic gadgets, dresses, shoes, watches, super market etc. Around 8km / 20 minutes by taxi, we suggest make a group of 4 and hire a taxi or if you are alone the cheap and best way is by underwater train service. The name of the station you need to get down is called Shanghai Science and Technology Museum stop. Please see below the map and information

Does the terminal have a free Wi-Fi? **No**
Nearest western union, money transfer facilities, money changers/forex from the terminal. Right out of terminal gate, **Bank of Agriculture. Also local people, do money exchange.**
Nearest shopping mall from where we are Docked is: **No.1018 Tang Shan road, 3km away from terminal. Not accept US dollar or Euro. 30 minutes by walking and 10 minutes by car. Please see the map**

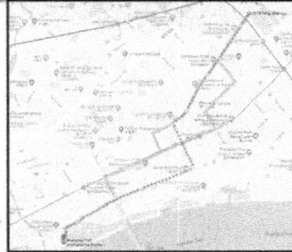

Columbus Crew Welfare Notice

Columbus Ps4 FIFA19 Champions League

1" place
The Columbus Ps4 FIFA 19 CHAMPION
YEVHENII
Entertainment Team
UKRAIN

2nd Place
STEFAN
Bar
SERBIA

3rd Place
MARIO
Photo
COLOMBIA

Also, where is the nearest Western Union, so the crew can send money home in case of emergencies?

Once I get this information, I post it in our Crew Daily Times, which I publish every day, so the crew can plan in advance. It is very similar to the passengers' daily Explorer, with information like which port are we in, and what time do we reach the port, and when do they need to be back on board?

Small reminders every day include: wash their hands as often as possible, be kind, speak English in all guest areas, safety training, sanitation training, a little bit of information about the port we will visit, and keep smiling.

If it's a sea day, the next day, then I will educate them on safety issues and how important safety on board is. The next time I might add a motivational article, like from Mother Teresa or history. We also do some fun facts, like a column called "Did You Know" with educational and fun facts about a country.

When crew members come on board, their first line of contact is with me. Once they reach the gangway, security calls me, and I am the one who welcomes them, which is why I am titled the Crew Ambassador.

First thing we do is go to the crew office and check that all their certifications are correct. So, it's usually 99% that is correct, and we approve, and we go forward. One person might have left something at the airport or back home.

Then, after that short orientation, I take them for lunch or dinner. I call the department buddies. Every department has a buddy. For example, say there is a group of cooks. The Chef has nominated one person to be the buddy from the galley, and that person would come down and take that group and show them around the ship.

It's a very busy day coming up in Singapore; we have 108 crew members joining the ship. If it's their first time on board a ship, we take special care of them; it can be hard being away from their family, boarding the new ship, not knowing anybody, finding their new cabin and cabin-mate, meeting a new team, new supervisor, new manager. It's very confusing to the new crew and me personally. I would rather take care of those first-time people on board. I segregate them after asking have you been on Columbus before. Your mentor is coming down, but any doubts now or in the future, just let me know, and I will tell them. On the second or third day I will do my training. Subjects are the do's and don'ts, but I focus a little bit more on the safety and sexual harassment.

Columbus Sports Fest 2019   CCW   **Doubles Dart Tournament**

AND THE
WINNERS
ARE...

501 Scoring

1st Prize
Katy/Lee
Ent

2nd Prize
Hannah/Craig
Ent

3rd Prize
Pavlo/Aleksander
HK

Congratulations to our Winners!!

1000 £ JACKPOT BINGO

10 £ = BINGO (4 TICKETS IN ONE) + POPCORN + SOFT DRINK / BEER

Charged to your onboard Account, So no need for cash.

WHERE: CREW MESS
WHEN: 22ND MARCH
TIME: 23:45 hrs (11:45 pm)

Matrix:- Single Bingo card will have 4 games on an A4 size paper. The games will be fully explained again and again to all the Crew members before the games will start.

• WE WILL PLAY **4** GAMES

• Prizes are as follows

1ST GAME = 50£   2ND GAME = 100£   3RD GAME = 150 £
4th and final game is called FULL HOUSE
JACKPOT (SURE WIN) = 400 £
We will play until someone will walk away with 400 GBP
If you get 24 numbers right in 40 call

Please get a pen with you for the bingo

All Prizes will be paid in CASH.
ON THE SAME DAY AT THE SAME TIME.

IT'S TIME TO GET RICH
AND GO
SHOOOOHPPPPINGGGGG IN
HONG KONG

You will take home a sum of **1000** in cash

If you get 24 numbers right on 45 calls you get 700 in cash
If you get 24 numbers right on 50 calls you get 500 in cash

Cards will be sold in the crew mess on the 22nd March (the day of the Bingo) from 2200hrs onwards

WISHING YOU ALL THE BEST
Together, we can make a difference

The most important thing is the company structure training. Who does what, when this company was started, and what are the expectations we have toward you?

So, these are the two basic trainings. Once we do this, I coordinate with the safety officer, and he needs to give them a safety briefing and a booklet about the regulations. It's mandatory by the International Maritime Organization that any time there are new crew and passengers on board, before the ship starts its engines and sails into the seas, the crew members need to know what their duties are. They will be trained in the next day or two on safety, but on CMV we prioritize that more than anything else. Even though they will get thorough training the next day, in case there was an emergency that first day, CMV wants everyone to know exactly what to do. I would show him exactly which lifeboat to go to, and what are his emergency duties. All of the 650 crew have different emergency duties. When there is a fire, not everybody runs to it. It's a team that goes to extinguish it. If the fire goes a little bit more, then we have a second, third and fourth stage, but every crew member needs to know their safety duties before they start to work, whether it's a waiter, a cleaner, a cook, the Captain or the Hotel Director.

"How can the crew communicate with others back home?"

Basic communication is Wi-Fi, because Wi-Fi offers you a visual audio like with Facebook, Skype or WhatsApp. It's available in the crew bar. They get a card for whatever amount of data transmission they want to buy. The ship's Wi-Fi on board works on data, not on time. So, what I do is type all my messages and keep them ready to copy. The moment I connect, it sends them, and then I log off. If you are smart, you can save on data and save your background updates for when you log on in port, where you have free Wi-Fi. There are some people who are texting all the time. They have Wi-Fi cameras connected back home so they can speak and say hi how are you all the time.

And when we are in port, every two or three days, there is always Wi-Fi in a coffee shop or restaurant. I think the Wi-Fi is quite good on Columbus. I see a lot of video chats especially late at night when the load is lighter and the system is at its best. The passengers are not using it, and that is when the crew uses it. The Asian time zone means that everybody back home is awake when it's midnight on the ship. We've never had any issues with communication.

"Some religions have practices, like Muslims, etc., so how does that work with the crew?"

When crew have special needs for their religious practices, we have made special arrangements for the food when the time comes, and we give them a special place with mats that they can all come together and do their prayers.

It's Easter right now for the Christians, and we are celebrating the Way of the Cross every Friday in our little prayer room. We are very focused on the Muslim group who eat no pork. We have designed the menu in such a way that they always have other options. Even during the crew parties, the food is designed with an international menu. We also satisfy the Indians and the Ukrainians, who are a major part of our crew, with Indian curries and Russian borscht. We include international dishes like fried chicken, burgers, hot dogs, and ice cream as well. Yesterday was a crew party, so the Chef sent the menu to me. If I want to add something, we talk it over, and our first priority is the guest, but if he has something extra, then we design the menu accordingly.

CMV is quite good about vacation times. The crew are on vacation for two to four months. If you request for a holiday well in advance, and if you have an occasion when you need to be home, we let you choose, and we try our best to give you what you want.

Columbus Crew Welfare Notice

Table tennis Championship: - Part of the Columbus Sports fest 2019

Congratulations to all the winners!

The best 3 out of 32 contestants Bravo!!!!!

Prizes: 1st prize 1GB SHIP INTERNET VOUCHER
2ND Prize 500MB SHIP INTERNET VOUCHER
3RD Prize power bank

1st Prize

Columbus Champion

Yudha
Deck

2nd Prize

Bobi
Housekeeping

3rd Prize

Pasek
Photo

The Columbus Daily Good News

MONDAY 25TH MARCH 2019   **PORT:** Halong Bay , Vietnam

QUOTE OF THE DAY

."*DISCIPLINE IS CHOOSING BETWEEN WHAT YOU WANT NOW AND WHAT YOU WANT MOST.*"

WHATS TODAY

Halong Bay , Vietnam : In Vietnamese, Ha Long means "descending dragon." Halong Bay is a beautiful natural wonder in northern Vietnam near the Chinese border. The Bay is dotted with 1,600 limestone islands and islets and covers an area of over 1,500 sqkm. This extraordinary area was declared a UNESCO World Heritage Site in 1994. For many tourists, this place is like something right out of a movie.

Crew information
There is no Wi-Fi in the terminal. The money exchange is available inside the Sun world Park and city centre..5 min. There are some small shopping malls along the walking street, they are outside the gate and near the port. We recommend VINCOM HA LONG, about 6.8km far from the park, if you are looking for wider choice and extensive shopping.

TODAY IN THE MESSES

Lunch

Pork Soulaki

Dinner

Punjabi Dal

WHAT TO SEE

Hang Sung Sot Cave is located at Bon Hon Island
Cat Ba Island is the most popular attraction
Monkey Island is also known as Cat Dua in Vietnamese
White sandy beaches and there are a plethora of activities on offer here.

COMING SOON

Crew Party : 29th March, in the Dome.
Movie and popcorn night : Dates.to be Announced.
Dart competition : Dates to be announced

WEATHER ☀

Skies:	cloudy
Temperature:	22°C
Sunrise:	05:55 AM
Sunset:	18:06 PM

PORT OF CALL

Arrival:	07:00 HRS
All on Board:	22:00HRS
Departure:	23:00HRS
Currency	Vietnamese dong

HAPPY BIRTHDAY

Dimas Konstantinos
A/C Engineer

EMERGENCY CONTACT

Ship's Tel.: +87 0773910310

DRILL

NA

CREW AMBASSADOR

Please see the crew ambassadors for AVOs
Office Hours : 10:00 - 15:00 / 17:30 -23:30
Tel : 7476 / Beeper 581 / Radio Ch.3
For Urgent matter available 24/7

DO NOT FORGET

Please be advised that TODAY is the last day for the Wire Transfer for this month .

Any kind of cigarettes, including open one's, are prohibited by Singapore Customs regulations and will be subject for fine plus confiscation. For transferring crew to Vasco Da Gama the whole ruling applies as well.

We always give crew members two choices for coming back to work. Either they take the dates we give them, which is two or three months of vacation, or, if they need five months, then they take the next available date after that five months, meaning it might be six months. When you are on vacation you are not being paid. CMV is flexible, and they can decide.

"You get an idea that even though you are of a different nationality, you are going to be welcomed?"

The majority of people, when you ask what would you prefer, 1) to work in a diverse environment

> A guest is looking at the photographs displayed and asks, "How will I know which ones are mine?"

or 2) would you rather work with a majority of one nationality, would choose #1. I believe 99% would say they want to work in a diverse environment.

The problem is, when you have a majority, the drawback is, they wouldn't use English. The majority of the crew would not use English as their main language for communication, and that is not good for us because we are here for the guests. The guest is the bread and butter. We suggest:

"You don't get better in English if you don't use it."

For that matter, I forget my own language; when I go back home, I have a big struggle, and my kids make fun of me. The language name is spelled the same if you write it reversed. Either way it is spelled Malayalam. It has 56 letters in its alphabet compared to 26 in the English language. It's from the southern tip of India in Cochin, one of the ship's ports.

"Other than missing their family for the new people coming aboard, what is the hardest thing for new crew to adapt to?"

We all have our different priorities. For some it might be food, because I believe the best chef in the world is your own mother. That would be the first challenge. For some, maybe they miss their own country and the environment where they grew up.

Out of the ship's windows, all you see is the blue waters, and that might cause a challenge. Then, coming from an environment where diversity is not around, and you don't have your own people, suddenly you come to places where people are different; differences include the language, food, religion, body language, entertainment, and even the different TV channels.

Fortunately, 90% of the crew coming here have worked on ships before, but my focus on the first day is on those who have never worked on a ship before. I know many years ago, when I first came on board, I had the same concerns. So, I have empathy and can step into their shoes and think what their mentality is.

"What about privacy in their room. Do they mind having a roommate?"

No, the majority never say they want to change their cabin because they can't get along with their cabin mate.

But we can change their cabin. We let them choose like-minded people. That is normal, even back home. Sometimes two good people cannot make two good friends.

> The reason why the sailors aren't playing cards is that the Captain is standing on the deck.

Each department has a block of cabins. We do that, because the starting times are similar. Like the deck will start at 6:00am and have set break times. When they finish their duties, they might have three or four hours of free time, and then by 9:00pm they might go to bed. However, if you look at a bar guy, he might start working at twelve noon and end up working till three or four in the morning.

Housekeeping also has a standard time starting at 7:00 in the morning with a break from 1:30pm to 5:00pm and finish work at 9:30pm. They might socialize for one or two hours before bedtime. The cabin mate won't have a problem with coming in and out, showering, or napping. All the cabins are shared by two, with some cabins having an extra bed that can be used to store luggage.

Officers, if on the privilege list, have a single cabin. When there is a problem with cabin mates, we try to find out what the problem is, and sort it out by changing the cabins or counseling/coaching the other crew member who is the challenge.

Most of the cabins have refrigerators, and all have telephone and TVs. Many cabins have a DVD player and USB reading device. All crew have their own cell phones and many have gaming devices.

"There is a book called, *The Customer Comes Second*. If the employees are happy, then the passengers are going to be happy."

Definitely, which is why the motto on board is, "Happy Crew Makes Happy Guests. Happy Guests and Crew Make a Happy Ship".

We want, daily, everyone who steps out of their cabin and steps into their workplace to be happy. We just want them to ask. This is what we say in the orientation; if the smallest of things trouble you, come and try us. Maybe we cannot resolve all of the problems, but maybe it will make your heart a little easier, and you'll have somebody to talk to. I am your neighborhood Spiderman, and I'll try my best to resolve the issues and make you smile and happy.

"Is it natural that all the people we see in the halls are always greeting others with a smile and hello, how are you today?"

That is what we expect from them. They are told this in the Customer Service orientation in the beginning, which is part of what is injected into them with the dos and don'ts.

The first day on board is the safety drill, and then comes their comfort and the welcome kit. They have so much to do with meeting their new cabin mate, and after that is taken care of comes the orientation. This is part of the service of meeting and greeting guests according to the time of day, using eye contact and saying sorry, or apologize, if necessary.

Galley to dining room escalator

"How long does it take for a waiter to be trained to go up and down that escalator?"

Actually, when you look, it looks very difficult. It's like when you see somebody riding a bicycle, I would look at him and say, oh my gosh, it has two wheels, and how is he balancing? It looks so hard. But once you learn to ride a bike or motorbike, you are not even balancing it; you are just riding it. It's using basic physics.

If you balance it properly and know the right procedure, that training is done by the mentors on the restaurant team. People like Subhash or the Maître 'D have special training for specific jobs. Carrying the tray is done in such a way that he is not carrying ten or twelve plates at one time. He starts by carrying one, then two, then four, etc. The techniques of where to put your hand are taught. The closer you put your hand to your shoulder, the less weight you will have. Farther away from your shoulder makes the tray

Color coding distinguishes roles

heavier.

Even in the orientation, we have heavy objects, so we can train the right procedure to lift; you always keep your legs together and bend your knees, so you don't put the pressure on your back. Your legs can take more pressure than your back. And always keep the thing next to your chest. If you don't train your crew properly, back injuries can be a big problem. So that is on our priority list.

We always teach them about something we call PPE or Personal Protective Equipment. If a galley steward is going to wash a grill, he has to make sure he is wearing an apron, safety glasses, and two pairs of gloves. The inner pair are yellow, covered by the outer pair, which come up to his elbows. Hygiene and sanitation are also on CMV's priority list. He takes care of these things himself.

The motto for safety is, "Your safety is your priority".

The waiter is taught balance in trying to carry the trays but also posture, so he doesn't damage his back. Even if talking with a friend, movement on the escalator doesn't increase or decrease; it's already calculated in your mind. Timing on the escalator becomes something the waiter can do, even if he is sleeping, because he is used to that, as it's his daily route.

"Tell us about the green and red scarves the crew wear when preparing the food."

Every company follows a particular color coding, so we don't need to ask if someone is a Chef de Cuisine, a Chef de Partee, a Sous Chef, or an Assistant Cook. Looking at the color coding, we come to know who is in charge of the galley. Now

> What would happen if I flushed the toilet while sitting on it?

the production center, (which is the main galley located on deck six and has the hot and cold sections, as well as the pantry, bakery, and pastry), is all under one roof. Those who wear the green scarf are called a First Cook. The First Cook has one or two assistants under him who are wearing red scarves. Under them are the 3rd Cooks wearing white scarfs. All sections are headed by a Chef Tournant who wears an orange scarf.

They are fully in charge of the galley, and above them come the Sous Chefs. We have a Sous Chef in each outlet; the Plantation has its Sous Chef, and the main galley has a Sous Chef. The same level are the baker and the pastry chef, like Neil, who is in charge of all the cold pastries, and the baker is in charge of all the bread.

All the production is done in the main galley on deck six; food is taken up to the Plantation or the Bistro. There are smaller pantries where you can heat up food if it is precooked. But the timing tells when to bring it up, and there are logs as to what to get. The Sous Chef has this responsibility on his back. The whole thing is headed by Shone Matthew, who is the Executive Chef.

"Can you tell me any funny stories between guests and crew?"

They are like passing clouds, they just pass away. I have noticed as a waiter how much I loved the long cruise because of the personal bonding with the guests, and still, I write to some of them.

Couples always ask for a table for two. But people who have cruised a lot would prefer a table for eight so they can talk to different couples.

There was one waiter who is on Magellan right now, but he always stood by the door. I never had seen him stressed, but always smiling. Always a

> Topless sunbathing should be banned. My husband spent all day at the beach, people watching, and didn't get his errands done.

happy-go-lucky Santa Claus guy, but never takes anything seriously, which was one of his drawbacks. He had a big huge stomach, and when he sneezed, the buttons would fly away. He used to rest his hands right on his stomach. A funny looking guy: a nice cartoon. We dressed him up as Santa Claus every Christmas, so he was the standard Santa Claus for the crew. I would give him chocolates to go around from the Crew Captain, and he was always there for birthday parties, because he had a very loud and clear voice, so he didn't need a microphone.

So, this guest comes and stands there in this big line for open seating, and they all want a table for two, and they are all gone. *"We are completely packed, even a table for eight,"* he says. The couple ask again for a table for two, and he says, *"Madam, have a look; it's so thickly packed that I cannot offer you a table, so you might have to wait for five or ten minutes."*

So, the guest is very upset and says she wants a table for two. *"Yes, looking at the sequence, I will get you a table, but it might be five to ten minutes"* he says again.

He is looking around in an upset way and comes up with an idea. What he does is says to the couple, *"A table for two, right, and by the window, and you are sure? Just give me a minute."* He took some paper, and took out his pen, drew a nice window, and a two-table and handed it the man and said, *"Here you go sir; here is your nice window, and you can see an eagle flying in the sky and your table and two chairs."*

Laundry Team Smiles

The guests were so happy they were laughing all day long. They even laughed in their cabin for more than a week, thinking about this guy and how he explained it to them.

Another story happened while we were cruising the Alaska fjords, and there you get to see a lot of wildlife, like the dolphins, seals, and the blue whales making the big fountains.

All of a sudden, somebody sees a group, like six or seven dolphins, and everybody rushed toward that window. And I know it's just a one-minute thing, and either the ship is too fast or the dolphins are too fast. But there was an old lady who was struggling to get up, and she had a walking stick, and she reached the window and couldn't see the dolphins, and she was very sad. Another waiter comes over and says, what happened madam; why are you so sad?

"I wanted to see the dolphins on my cruise, and everybody saw them, but because of my problem I could not see," she said. He said to her, don't worry; what is it you want to see, dolphins? So, he takes a big picture of dolphins

hanging outside the restaurant and puts that in front of her, and says, okay, just imagine this is how beautiful the dolphins are. He even named each of the dolphins. She was so happy and laughing.

The waiter said, *"If I were a little better, I could make the time go backwards and sit you closer to the window where they saw the dolphins. However, next time I see the dolphins, I am going to call you and carry you, but for now: [and he moved the picture up and down for her to enjoy.]"*

All of the guests treated that guest very kindly for the rest of the cruise, and all of us waiters would always give her a table near the window. She did get a chance to watch the whales and the dolphins from her window. *"That is an example of what the Guest Relations Officer was talking about, when he said, there is no such word as 'no'. That is what they did, being creative in their response."*

We tell the crew members to not use words like 'no', it is impossible; it is not there. We say, we'll give it a try and get back to you later. And if it really is impossible, we say right now we don't have it, but we will make it available in

> *Two new recruits were on the deck of a ship. One turns to other and says, "It's awfully quiet on deck tonight. Isn't it? "Other recruit replies, "Everyone must be watching the band." First one, "There is no band on this ship." Reply, "No, I definitely heard the Captain say, a band on ship."*

the next few days. Or we give them other options. We try to never say 'no', and instead try to be creative, because nothing is impossible. We have a thing about diversity, so it's not like all we do is give them parties. Some like parties, but others get sports fests, because some people are keener on playing sports. They like fitness, so we give them clean working equipment. We give them the table tennis, the pool table, darts, chess, foosball, PS4, and, for those who want to pray, we have the chapel and prayer room.

One year back we started this position of Crew Ambassador. It was Jakob Kummer's idea along with Elian Clauss, the Hotel Director. Jakob controls the Crew Ambassador, he monitors us, and we report to him. On the ship, the Hotel Director is the boss and who I report to. The first Crew Ambassador was Ritesh, and they said he has a few programs in place, so try and learn from him. We each did our own things of what we could do with what we had on each ship with the resources we have. We work hand in hand and are in constant contact, and sharing is caring, so we share our new ideas. We put everything in one box and take out what works. We are still in the growing stage, but we are getting there.

CHAPTER FORTY-EIGHT

🎁 *Crew Ambassador: Ritesh Fernandes: India*

The more you give, the more you get

The following is a summary of an interview with a Crew Ambassador who returned to the ship CMV Columbus in 2019 in relief of his predecessor, Joseph

(knick-named, "Baby"), who served during the vacation break for Ritesh.

It's just Columbus that I've done with this company. This is my third contract. We started off with the crew program in January, 2018

"The goal is to have an Ambassador on each of the six ships?"

They are trying as much as they can, but probably on a

Guest Services Manager and Ritesh

real small ship it would be difficult. The main goal is to have someone to take care of the crew from the day they join. They need to feel welcome, because the first few days initially are the most difficult time for anyone. No matter how many years you've been working on the ship, when you come for the first few days on a new ship, it's always challenging, because you are just coming back from vacation where your mind is relaxed. You will have different things to do over here. It's not just a job.

I always say to the crew members: first comes safety; then comes the job, then comes your leisure and the pleasure of entertainment. When you come here, you have more responsibilities. It's not just reporting for duty on time, like seven

> We had to queue outside
> with no air-conditioning.

o'clock. You have other things to take care of. Maybe there's an emergency signal you have to attend to.

On land, it is different. Here we have different rules. For example, in certain areas you're not allowed to wear flip flops as crew members, because it's for your safety. Especially in the M-1 (main corridor on crew deck) where you have the provisions and loading happening. There are cranes and heavy stuff we pick up. You need to wear shoes. Safety is always first, so this is what we try to get them oriented to from the first day. What to know and where to go. At least they know where to have a meal, and to whom they report. This program is a good thing, and I think it's nice.

"What is the biggest thing that has changed from 2 or 3 years ago to now?"

Their welfare is there, but it could be the smallest issues. For example, we help if something's not working in their cabin, and they can report it to me. I normally have enough time to follow up that it's being done. They used to have to report to reception, but they have to cater to the customers first. There might be delays, and they can't just keep calling reception every time. There is a request form, and if I am not around, there is a box they can just drop it in. We try to get the requests done that day, especially if it has to do with the toilet not working or a light needing repair. If it's a broken chair, something for the carpenter, and not urgent, then we handle it when we can. On issues with the food, someone has to keep a quality check on the food and beverages in the crew mess. Earlier, they couldn't say it to anyone, if they didn't like it; it might be because you are not going to get the same exact food you have at home. We have to keep in mind the different nationalities. There might be something you like. If you don't eat pork, there will be something else.

There will be something if I'm a vegetarian. If they don't like something, or it's not tasting nice, they can tell me, and I can speak to the chef. These are the small issues where we can help, because maybe they feel they cannot speak to their supervisors or feel intimidated. After they speak to me, I can go and say, in a nice way, is there some way we can have this done for this person?

M/V COLUMBUS

Employee of the month awards

Maybe it's just to smooth the process. You won't see a Crew Ambassador wearing [military-like] stripes. In general, when the crew member sees someone wearing stripes, it is a totally different idea, and you show respect. They can just come and talk to me as a friend. I also give crew members personal advice or suggestions. It is not just about do this or do that. When they're going on a vacation, I always tell them you have three months; the best way to utilize them, if you want to grow, is learn a new language.

I try to tell them, get experience. I started in 2006 from the smallest position, because in India, no matter what experience you have, you need to start from the lowest. I started to be a galley cleaner, but in two years over there, I got one of the biggest promotions. One minute, I was a person cleaning the galley, and in the next contract, I'm sitting right next to the captain and having a meal, because I was entitled to the officer's mess.

I was in entertainment, like DJ-ing and events. That was just a hobby that I had. I was a restaurant manager for a hotel, called Alfredo's in Mumbai. Different positions give you that experience, and I feel really happy. I can share this with new crew, and this is a way I can motivate them.

When I joined this ship at the opening, I joined as an assistant waiter. No matter the years of experience or what position I was last holding when I was offered this, I was ready to take it, because they said, I know you will go ahead, and you will reach where you want to be.

I came as assistant waiter. From day one, if you have a focus, and you know what you're here for; if you want to grow, if you give it a shot, it's definitely going to work. This is what I always tell them, just do your best. There will be a lot of things around you, especially if you worked a higher position; then it might be a little hard to grasp for you, but your focus is very important. I always tell them to work hard; the company's growing, and you can grow. I'm a living example for you. I was in the restaurant with some of you guys. If you want to grow, just do your best.

That's how you motivate them; they're going to stay on the same page. It's not always blue skies. Sometimes it's going to rain, sometimes sunny. You have to take it the way it comes.

I always tell them try to speak in English, not their mother tongue. If you don't speak, you will never learn. You have to try, even if it's broken English. One crew member could understand English, but he spoke very broken English when he joined. I just saw him now a few months later, and he is speaking very good English.

I always say try; even if you are incorrect, someone will correct you, so you can learn. They might not actually speak, but they have to understand and use it for reports, because, in an emergency, that's the only language we use.

"What do you do to make the crew feel like they are part of this family?"

We have a lot of events happening. It's not just work and more work. I told them, maintain a balance. We try to have different events. We might have a movie night; for someone who doesn't go to the bar every time, we might have a sports event. We have the foosball tournament happening soon. Some people love tennis, so they play table tennis. My first target is to put a library in, and I'm trying to put more books in

Crew friends cooking together at BBQ

there every time.

Most of the time, I'm not just sitting in the office near the crew area. I try to be more present when they're having their meal times. I just stay around there to talk to them. If they feel comfortable, I might even be in the Crew Bar sometimes, at the end of the night, to see things inside; I meet a lot of crew members whom I will not meet during the day. They are more comfortable about talking over there. They might not have time to walk to the office and tell me something important. It's better to be present out there; the office work and emails will always be in the office; communication is very important. And that connection has to be there, so they feel warm. I want to see all of them just to remind me.

"How does the crew know they are doing their job well?"

The first thing we tell them, if you have any doubts, you always ask; sometimes, you have to be open to different ideas. The supervisor might have something different in mind, and you have to listen to him or her. If you have views or ideas, you can always share. We have the Employee-of-the-Month award, which is in one way it motivates them. It's not just the small amount of money that's given as a gift. It's an honor.

Soup kettle now ready to go

It's a way to work a little extra to put in a little more. Everyone wants to be Employee-of-the-Month. The pictures are always posted around. That gives them that extra push where they want to do a little more.

"Are there any things you put together for the crew?"

Apart from the team nights, once each week, we have a disco night for the crew members in the crew bar. It's a different theme every time. We celebrate different holidays, because we have 27 nationalities on board. It might be a festival that they have back home.

"How many of those festivals each year?"

Just the important ones, which we can accommodate. Independence Day or something like that. That's what is more important. What they like to celebrate, I mean, are a lot of festivals, but you cannot do all of them. Now we have Easter, and on that same day we have a team night, so we can have an Easter bowl for them. They can also celebrate, because it's going to be a busy day, and they're going to be serving a lot of things for the passengers. At the same time, they know when they come back after work, at least they have something.

Once a month, we have a designated day for a birthday bash. They can buy something from the crew bar, like a free drink, alcoholic or non-alcoholic, and we try to have a cake cutting. I personally deliver the birthday cards to each one of them. They are signed by the captain. It has a small note saying happy birthday. Now everyone knows it is their birthday. We try and put it in our daily program which makes them feel good. I try to deliver the card when they are working, so everybody around knows it is their special day.

"Can you think of any random acts of kindness?"

I had a crew member who joined first time on the ship, and he was totally new; he was feeling lost for a few days. And the first thing he said to me was, I want to go home. He was feeling seasick. I used to go where he was working and say, I'll tell your supervisor, and he suggests you take a break for some time.

He said, I miss my wife and my family. And I said, what is the reason you are here?

Why did you take this job? And he said, I have to support my family. And I also reminded him of the time and cost that went into getting him on board; it might take three to six months to get hired, and there's some time and money that you invested for doing the courses that are required to get things done. I just reminded him, and I said, while you were home, you

One fashion conscious cruiser complained that her life vest didn't match any of her shoes.

didn't have a job. You need to keep an account of what you have spent, the hard work, and the decisions that you took. We were all here for the first time, and it was difficult for me the first two days; I was the new guy, and I told him I was sea sick. I gave him my phone, and I said, you can talk to your family whenever you want to. He called, started to get it, and now, he's working; he's fine. Absolutely. And they thank me, and his wife is grateful there was someone to guide him, and just give him that direction; the first few days are difficult.

You might feel homesick; it might be stress. Some people are a bit depressed, because that's what I tell them. Do not isolate yourself in the first few days. Try to get out of your comfort zone, meet people, try to speak. And then they get used to it. He did not drink, but he would always come to the crew bar, have a coffee, play a game, or play foosball. These are the things which mean personally touching someone where you know they could make the decision which could go wrong in the future, and they realize like, "If it were not for you, I would have already gone home, and I've changed my decision."

It's just the counseling that you give to the crew members, because they know that you've been in this position. They have this connection level. It was easier for me, because they saw me working in the restaurant earlier. Now they feel more comfortable, because they know I have done the job that they were doing. I am not some boss, and I don't want to be someone where I am looking down at them. I'm always with them, like having a meal with them. It is just that connection that you create. Communication. It can change someone's life. Just communicate; that's really important.

"What are some things you don't do regularly?"

We go to Norway; we have these football tournaments. There's a football ground just outside the gangway, like five minutes just across. This is something that would be different from what we do regularly. We tried to find out if there's a basketball court; in Bergen, if you go, they have a basketball place. Some of them like to play.

"Can you sense a difference in attitude from two years ago?"

When we first opened the ship, everything was new. There was no direct flow: not a straight line. Everybody had their own view, and now they are on the same page. For example, ten people come from ten different companies with ten different ideas. A standard was set and gradually everyone gets on the same page.

"You've worked on other cruise lines; how does this one compare?"

Every company is different. I would not look at the ups and downs but more at the advantages that I have. Each company up-rooted something. That is a part of where I am today. At CMV, it's homier than other places, I would say. I realized the smaller the ship the more like a family. I worked on a ship with 1500 crew, and it might take days to see someone because of the duty timings and the cabin locations. You might meet on disco night and not see them again for a month. It is impossible to interact with each and every one, whereas on this ship you meet every individual. It is easier to feel relaxed here and to get to know people from all departments.

"So, you are always thinking of new things to try?"

Yes, if I had to eat the same food every day, I would not like it. I would like some variation. We try to listen if someone has friends from other companies with ideas, and they say, why not here.

"So, it seems you are saying yes to new ideas?"

It depends if I get the approval. Another thing I am trying to start which will be a difficult challenge for me. We have the crew party once a month where we serve free alcohol but it is always late at night. My idea is to have a day party for those people who work at night. Just something special for them so they have something to feel they are not being left out and are being included.

When I was smaller, my mom would tell me, "The more you give, the more you get". The bottom line of where it comes from. A few years ago, Winston Churchill said, *"We make a living by what we have, but we make a life by what you give"*.

Salad anyone?

Winners of the World cruise Crew Raffle 2019

1st Prize £ 500

MUHAMMAD NAJIB
Laundryman
Housekeeping

2nd Prize

ALINA STXFAROVA

Dancer/Entertainment

Huawei P20 Lite ANE-LX3 32GB Unlocked GSM Phone w/ Dual 16MP/2MP Camera - Midnight Black

3rd Prize

VOLODYMYR LYSENKO

Asst. Electrician/Engine

Huawei Y7 2018 L09-LX2 5.99" Snapdragon HSR 2GB RAM DUAL SIM A-GPS Fingerprint
- 5.99" HUAWEI Y7 full view Display (1440x720)
- 2GB+16GB
- Rear Camera: 13MP/ Front Camera: 8MP +Selfie Toning Flash
- Fingerprint /8 Nano cards slot
- Battery: 3000mAh

5th,6th,7th,8th,9th,10th,11th,12th,13th,14th,15th,16th,17th,18th,19th and 20th

4th prize

Power bank 20000mah

Milan Milosavljevic; Housekeeping

CHAPTER FORTY-NINE

✿ *Chef: Sobin Balan Thalananiyil: India*

I learn more deeply from the ship

Soin Balan Thalananiyil knows India and its cuisine, so the on -oard specialty restaurant, Indian Fusion, was a natural for him to manage. When first stepping aoard the Columus, a guest might think that there is only one restaurant aoard, ut in fact, in addition to the uffet with its huge variety of offerings, there is an upscale alternative, overseen y its creative Head Chef. He offers a fusion menu with oth European and Indian gourmet dishes. This is Soin's third contract in a specialty restaurant. He worked in places like Meridian, a worldwide rand.

Sobin's Fusion Grill

"What do you like most aout your jo?"

Cooking! In a professional kitchen, there are many tasks, like paper work and cleaning. Every work is important. I'm really interested to cook, because my grandmother was a great cook, and at my home, I'm from a farmer family. My grandfather had around 30 workers on his land. My grandmother used to make food for them. We fed them and paid money for their work. My first chef was my grandmother, my teacher. I was interested in Indian cooking. Now I like to go to the European cuisine, and I like French and Italian. In hotels I did only the European cuisine. I needed to learn European dishes. I knew Indian cooking and the taste. If I became an Executive Chef, I needed to learn the taste of European cuisine. Now, for a change, I am taking care of the Indian fusion. It's a mixture of European and Indian.

"Do you think that all of the different cultures on the ship have influenced you?"

Of course. When I was in India, and I was 14, there were not too many nationalities. But here, I came on board, and I saw Romanian people, Ukrainians, and Indonesians. I came to know people that are friendly, interesting, and honest with us. It's all about our mentality. If you are good by heart, other people are good by heart. It doesn't matter which country, nothing. Good environment, good atmosphere. Everybody should smile at each other, love each other. Try to forget the problems, worries, sadness, everything. I belong to a Hindu family. I am interested in the culture of the Hindus. We can say all Indians are Hindus, because it is not a religion. It's a culture. In India, all Muslims or Christians or Hindus belong to Hindu culture.

"So that kind of warmth and friendliness is part of the Hindu religion?"

You can see all the books about India. You would not go forward making issue with other people, because the meaning of Hindu books is only one thing. Peace. If you read these books, you would not fight.

"What do you miss when you go home?"

When I'm on board, I feel I want to go home. When I'm home, I feel to come back. It's

Sobin loves his spices

a fact, because when we are working, I love my job. It's not that my work is hard. It's not, because of time. I miss my family. At home, my mother never allows me to cook. She is the boss. I will make a big mess in the kitchen. In the

hotel or on the ship, when we do something, we have plenty of people to clean, to assist us. At home we need to do the cutting, cooking, serving and cleaning.

"What do you think you learned from working on the ship?"

New things, like a big sea. Every place I worked, I learned something. On the ship we are giving more importance to the European cuisines. If you are passing through the Mexican area, we will make the Mexican, just so I can learn Mexican cuisine from here. If you are passing through a Spanish area, we will make Spanish paella. I learn more from the ship than the hotel.

Colorful dessert

"Can you give us an example of the Indian Fusion that people really like?"

The difficult thing I face in fusion is that some persons don't like too many spices. We found a solution, which is to make three gravies for each curry. Like if you're making a lamb curry, one milder version, one medium, one spicy, and we ask which one you prefer?

"What is your greatest strength?"

My confidence. Even if I don't know how to make one particular dish, I don't say 'no' to myself. I don't know, but I will try. That is my confidence.

"Does this cruise line give you the opportunity to learn new things?"

CMV gives freedom to grow. Laziness happens if there is no control with freedom. Like there should be control if you are cleaning. Clean it properly.

"What do you think motivates you to do your best job?"

What do I need for doing a good job? Just a pat on the back. For my workers, we support them. You know the backbone of the kitchen is cleaning like washing the pots. We support them; then they will get a special power from their heart to do something good for the company.

CHAPTER FIFTY

Head of Marketing: Mike Hall, UK

Create a pleasing atmosphere

There are a handful of people who saw the dream from the eginning, and Mike Hall was one of those. From one ship to more is a direct result of the team's efforts to design and market a product that will e a success. Mike is a road -gauge, open-minded, common sense person who has the high standards and patience necessary to help grow a company in any industry, and cruise lines can certainly test one's patience in dealing with weather and expectations.

Flagship of the fleet

It is a triute to top mana ement that many of the interviewees have re-
phrase in their own wor s the truism that without the success of each
memer of the team, the   uests will not return for more of the top level of
service an satisfaction that the workers strive to eliver.

Put another way, the oal of every worker an the lea ers is to create an
atmosphere that pleases every uest while keepin that pro uct affor ale,
fun, an even excitin .

The comine success of these efforts will create jos an promotion
opportunities as the cruise line ecomes known an expan s its fleet.

The team is responsile for the excellence of the pro uct. Mike Hall is
responsile for informin the worl that it is availale an worth
 iscoverin .

CHAPTER FIFTY-ONE

🎁 *Hotel Director: Elian Clauss: France*

Leadership: Strong empathy for crew

Elian Clauss is the corporate Hotel Director for CMV and all its ships. He is a strategic thinker, which is important to every crew member, because CMV is a growing business, and the addition of any new ship creates valuable opportunities for every crew member.

Elian and Jakob visiting from home office

A few of his thoughts are summarized below. He knows the market CMV has chosen to serve and knows the capabilities of the crews and their managers. Because CMV is a smaller, more focused, business, it has the opportunity to serve new markets as a somewhat specialized cruise line.

The world cruises appeal to retirees who have the time to spend away from home and business requirements. He has commented on the "perfect storm" for the older segment of the market, where instead of parents dropping off their children for their first school day, leaving the parents with a time when close supervision and care is not required, now the children are dropping off their parents in a "win-win" situation. The parents love the cruise, and their children aren't required to attend to their needs.

The result is that CMV needs to have some "enrichment" activities available to entertain and educate the guests during the four months or so of the circumnavigation, especially on "sea

> *A couple complained that the captain was rude because he did not wait two hours for them at a port even though they had left him a note explaining that they had too much to do.*

days". The cruise directors need to have a robust calendar of enticing events to satisfy the time on board. Of course, there is another calendar of interesting excursions to educate the guest about the ports of call. Elian understands all of that.

He states that the marketing targets can get complicated. He sees parents getting older, and it's not fun to see your parents getting older. No, he thinks it's actually helping the people to stay younger. The food is wonderful and healthful. The entertainment and the happy days are making them love life, and loving life in spite of living longer makes it easy to be adventurous, to be able to trust yourself. To do something. To be able.

Elian used to wonder how it is possible to make good use of such a short time on shore when stopping at various ports. But, in the extreme case, he described a slight exaggeration, but made the point. He remembers his time on the ship.

I was always complaining that we have only a short time in these eight hours. We have only two hours on the coach. But I think I remember I 'did' New York in two hours. New York was amazing, and I went out and saw it in one weekend. Cruising people, though, are different from normal people, I think. I mean, they like challenges, and they've loved the adventure of travel, and they are different from just people that stay at home.

So even though you might think that people are dropping off their parents, I think their parents want to be here. I think they like the choices of all of the different places and the things to do in each place. The son or daughter are really happy for the parents who are getting older. They have the medical support in case of medical accidents, and did not have to beg all the time.

Elian's parents were both captains. So even though coming on the ship was new for him as an employee, he knew the business from his parents. He then immediately turned to the crew experiences and told the story of a cruise line with the new hire from India who was given

> *A guest once asked the Captain to turn the engines off as they were too loud.*

his ticket to London. But he arrived with flip flops and no coat, and it was below zero at the time. He doesn't have a pound or a penny in his pocket. And then he comes on board, and he sees this huge challenge.

The point here is that Elian and every person on the CMV team is empathetic to the new hire, and also the experienced crew member, and they organize ways to make their welcome work. They now have a Crew Ambassador who attends to the physical and mental challenges with hands-on help, including help in contacting family to assure them of his safe arrival.

Elian is justly proud of their returning crew numbers. We have an 82% record for joining crew returning; that's high in this industry. Normally the industry is about 70 or 72%, but that depends. The last year we just achieved 82%, from 80.15%; it's going up.

For the employee, we want to avoid the pressure about financial performance. We make our money when the passengers come on board, and they book excursions. We are not depending so much on bar sales, and our employees don't need to sell as much.

On some other lines, you are getting a commission alternative. So, you need to sell, and you don't ask the passenger if he wants a cheap wine or inexpensive wine; you will bring always the expensive one. On the shore excursion, you have to show results. With them, you need to reach at least 80% of the ship's bookings before you start to get, for your team, a commission out of it. But that's something you cannot expect of our passengers. They won't spend large amounts per day on extras on the ship.

Our specialty is testing the no-fly concept. Our passengers just refuse to fly, and we are not good with flying. It was just not our clientele. We are looking for word-of-mouth advertisers that are absolutely thrilled with the cruise line. Our crew is a key to that happening.

We do some special things for our crew. Cash for wages is important, because the workers don't use banks. If you want, we can pay you in cash. Because, for example, people come in and say the bank system is so corrupt. I will accept the contract if I can get cash. We say, okay, we will do it. We have to deliver the cash.

To summarize the leadership pattern of CMV, these are people who start with a strong empathy for the crew and the programs to make the crew happy. And that happy crew has a mission to please the guests. And the numbers of both crew and guests returning would suggest that this strategy is working well.

The key for any business is the employee workforce which enables management to take advantage of many efficiencies of running a business where the customer is king, and the reputation for service is outstanding.

Conclusions

This is a book for everyone. We share a planet with nature and our fellow citizens. We each have a curiosity about both that translates into studying human nature and biological and physical nature. Each of us has the freedom to live our lives as we choose. The stories of the crew members aboard a floating resort are heart-felt expressions of people serving people. In the process they have a job that makes it possible for them to support their families, make new friends, and fulfill their dreams. They discover that although we each have different cultures, there is much to be learned from befriending those who are different in ways like gender, age, skin tones, religion, customs, religion, priorities, food preferences, language, lifestyles, and attitudes. If we can celebrate our friendships with folks that used to be in an "out group", excluded from our circle of communication, we have advanced in maturity, knowledge, and enrichment in our lives. And in addition, we are more likely to be successful in what we have chosen to do with our lives.

The crew members have learned that although they might have wished that everyone could be exactly like themselves, that is not realistic, so they learn to celebrate the differences. A traveler explores the world out of curiosity to see different ways to look at and do things. They also learn that teamwork is good for their career, makes for happy and cooperative successes, and is more fun than arguing about things that are not really important.

If nations could do as well, what a great planet this would be, with everyone being kind and helpful. So, dear reader, draw your own conclusions from these dozens of stories. You are free to choose your attitudes, because no one else can make that choice. Which choice will make you and your loved ones happier, and build better friendships?

The author is a photo-journalist who has traveled and recorded images of people in villages, large and small, doing their daily activities and pleasing travelers who are open to experiencing new ideas and customs. Enjoy a vicarious trip with her, celebrate your opportunities at work and play that make life interesting, and share your new attitudes and your discovery of friends that are "different". Our planet is full of interesting people and wonders of nature. Check out the author page for more adventures.

Author Page

Jackie Chase, [JackieChase.com, WorldTravelDiva.com, and CulturesOfTheWorld.com], has traveled to over 100 countries and specializes in staying in remote villages in order to use her keen observations and photo-journalism skills to share her insights with her reader fans. She has traveled alone, with a child, with family, and with friends; she has earned over 32 awards from international book contests from 2014 to date of printing; she shares with the public many of the travel secrets she has experienced in her book titled, *"How to Become an Escape Artist" A Traveler's Handbook.* The Handbook was tested for several years with students in a college evening class, and they soaked up Jackie's hints and the many ways to avoid disappointment, reduce expenses and frustrations, navigate the issues of visas, language, customs, currencies, accommodations, transportation, attitudes, danger, travel alone, and other problems all covered in over 190 segments in the book. It is up to date with nearly 100 click links to hard-to-find websites dealing with all aspects of travel, including finding companions.

Her *"All Hands Working Together" Cruise for a Week: Meet 79 Cultures* book treats cruising in a unique way to learn about cultures; the reader experiences personal contact with crewmembers from many of the 79 countries they represent, and from many skills they possess.

Jackie Chase has written definitive books on "People to Meet" in contrast to "Places to See". She convinces her readership to look beyond mountains, lakes and buildings to see world inhabitants of all continents as potential friends and shows how much we have in common. She shows how to bridge gaps created by custom and language in *"100 People to Meet before You Die: Travel to Exotic Places"*. This book, [as well as the others], are available in color, grayscale, and, with stunning images in eBooks that come to life on backlit screens. This anthology involves 12 countries and contains 321 of those story-telling images and award-winning prose about her adventures. For her fans of a particular country, she has twelve "singles" in print and in eBook format, plus at least one (Panama) translated into Spanish.

For children, from small up through teens, a "winner" of a book is *"Giraffe-Neck Girl" Make Friends with Different Cultures*. It is about a ten-year-old girl in Thailand who warms the hearts of young and old as she shares her different life and customs.

Jackie Chase's 2016 book, *"Walking to Woot" A Photographic Narrative Discovering New Dimensions for Parent-Teen Bonding* has won 17 international awards in the genres of Parenting, Young Adult Non-fiction, Multi-Cultural, Cover Design and Travel, and it contains both poetic descriptions and visual ones with its nearly 170 images of life with stone-age tribal warriors who haven't changed customs in a thousand years. The New Guinea unclothed villagers welcomed Jackie and her blond 14-year-old daughter to pig roasts, unusual customs, and dances. Jackie Chase loves to hear from her fans and to see copies of reviews they submit to the web. Contact her at:

JakartaMoon@hotmail.com

BOOKS BY JACKIE CHASE: 2014/16
How to Become an Escape Artist: A Traveler's Handbook (2014-6)
Giraffe-Neck Girl: Make Friends with a Different Culture (2014)
100 People to Meet before You Die: Travel to Exotic Cultures (2014-6)

AWARDS (15) FOR THE FOUR BOOKS LISTED ABOVE
Royal Palm Literary Award; National Indie Excellence Book Award; FAPA President's Book Award; Readers' Favorite Book Award; International Book Award; USA Best Book Award; Beverly Hills Book Awards

AWARDS (17) For: *"Walking to Woot"* A Photographic Narrative
Discovering New Dimensions for Parent-Teen Bonding:
Beach Book: & San Francisco: Festivals; Beverly Hills Book Award in 3 Genres; Eric Hoffer Grand Prize Award in 2 Genres; Florida Authors and Publishers Association (FAPA, including cover award); International Book Award, Montaigne Medals; National Indie Excellence Award; Next Generation Indie Book Award in 2 Genres; Paris Book: Festival; Reader's Favorite Award in 3 Genres.

BUSINESS BOOKS BY JACKIE CHASE: 2017 and 2019 (This one)
'24-7' Multi-Cultural Workers Find Diversity Recipe to Heal a Troubled World
[Sharing inclusion/diversity ideas with employees/students/managers in businesses, charities and governments using inexpensive eBook distribution methods to reach every participant in the organization].

For further information click on link below:

www.AdventureTravelPress.com

Notes:

www.ingramcontent.com/pod-product-compliance
Lightning Source LLC
Chambersburg PA
CBHW031931190326
41519CB00007B/486